GONZO
CAPITALISM

ALSO BY CHRIS GUILLEBEAU

The Art of Non-Conformity

The $100 Startup

The Happiness of Pursuit

Born for This

Side Hustle

100 Side Hustles

The Money Tree

GONZO CAPITALISM

HOW TO MAKE MONEY IN AN ECONOMY THAT HATES YOU

CHRIS GUILLEBEAU

Little, Brown Spark

New York Boston London

Little, Brown Spark
Hachette Book Group
1290 Avenue of the Americas, New York, NY 10104
littlebrownspark.com

First Edition: August 2023

Little, Brown Spark is an imprint of Little, Brown and Company, a division of Hachette Book Group, Inc. The Little, Brown Spark name and logo are trademarks of Hachette Book Group, Inc.

The publisher is not responsible for websites (or their content) that are not owned by the publisher.

The Hachette Speakers Bureau provides a wide range of authors for speaking events. To find out more, go to hachettespeakersbureau.com or email HachetteSpeakers@hbgusa.com.

Little, Brown and Company books may be purchased in bulk for business, educational, or promotional use. For information, please contact your local bookseller or the Hachette Book Group Special Markets Department at special.markets@hbgusa.com.

ISBN 978-0-316-49127-3
Library of Congress Control Number: 2023939525

Printing 1, 2023

LSC-C

Printed in the United States of America

Human desire is not an autonomous process, but a collective one. We want things because other people want them.

— René Girard

———————

If I'm fake I ain't notice cause my money ain't.

— Nicki Minaj

Contents

Chapter One

The Money Revolution

CONCEPT: Money has always been more about perception than reality. If enough people decide that money is worth something, then suddenly it is! Recently, however, the understanding of money has become more distorted—and interesting—than ever before.

At some point in recent history, the global economy stopped making sense.

People everywhere began to think about money much differently than they had before. Figuring out what it all meant would take some time, but the early signs were impossible to miss.

For one thing, hundreds of thousands of people with no background in finance suddenly began day-trading the stock options of failing companies. *On purpose.* That last part was key: they knew there was no good reason for the stock prices of the companies they traded to rise. But rise they did, and they *kept* rising, frustrating the professional investors who'd taken out positions betting that the failing companies would, you know, fail.

Amateur investors earning large amounts of money by betting on failing companies was just one symbol of how the economy was shifting. OnlyFans, a social network that consisted largely of adult performers selling access to intimate videos, took off—and exhausted healthcare workers and elementary school teachers burned out from teaching virtual kindergarten suddenly discovered a *much* more profitable way to make a living.

As the platform grew, so did the moral panic. In response, the CEO announced that sex work would soon be banned on the platform—which was a problem, because the whole business was *built* on sex work. He eventually backed down at the demand of many of the performers, some of whom were earning far more than they ever would in a more conventional job. As one adult creator put it, "I make videos that you jerk off to. Why *shouldn't* I get paid?"

And then, of course, there was crypto. Cryptocurrency would change the world, *dude,* and make us all rich in the process. At one point, the price of a single Bitcoin rose to almost $69,000. This happened the same month in which the S&P500 stock market index had declined. Meanwhile, as token prices were at their highest in history, the bestselling "non-fungible" (meaning unique, one of a kind, but in digital form) tokens (NFTs) on the largest blockchain network were *drawings of apes.* Some of these images sold for $1 million or more—all for a single JPEG. Even the price of gold—a currency as old as time—saw a 25 percent spike. The value of all these assets, it seemed, had become completely untethered from their real-world value—and from the rest of the economy.

None of it made any sense, at least as long as you applied the old ways of thinking. Many people jumped on the bandwagon, while many others declared it a bubble, and dismissed it entirely. Whichever camp you fell into, one thing was clear: it was time to start thinking differently about how money works.

This book is about thinking differently.

———

You know what happened starting in the spring of 2020. There was a pandemic, it was bad, it changed everything.

What matters for our story is what happened next.

Restaurants, bars, and brick-and-mortar retailers emptied out. Travel ground to a halt. Schools and offices were closed, and many companies announced layoffs, job cuts, and furloughs. The federal government stepped in to stop the bleeding, and billions of dollars in stimulus money flooded the country.

Contrary to expectations, the economy didn't shrink, it grew. Housing prices skyrocketed. Economists suddenly began worrying about a *savings glut*—in other words, they were worried that people weren't spending enough of their disposable income.

Flush with cash, the percentage of Americans who invested in cryptocurrency doubled in a year. Uber drivers were suddenly talking about something called altcoins. Prisoners, who received stimulus payments along with everyone else, began betting on stocks with their newfound wealth.

For more than a year, Bitcoin climbed higher and higher as investors poured in. So did shares in Tesla, Peloton, and plenty of other tech companies. Though these assets eventually came back down to planet Earth, a sea change in perception had set in. As some of the investors in failing companies put it, "Stocks only go up."

"The government can't just keep printing money!" a surprisingly small number of people said during this time. But it did.

A new meme explained these trends in even simpler terms: *Money printer go brrrrrr.*

It was as though all the old rules had gone out the window and money was falling from the sky. And nothing that happened later—not record inflation, high gas prices, or media reports of crypto exchange collapses—seemed to fully reverse the mindset that had taken hold.

Money: It's Whatever You Want It to Be

Let's back up slightly. Where does money come from, anyway? From the money fairy, of course. Or, technically, it comes from the government, which decides which types of money it should issue and how much should be printed.

But is it really that simple? Of course not... or, wait. Actually, *it is* that simple.

That is exactly how it works: the government prints money whenever it wants, and most of the time, the people accept that it's worth whatever they're told.

Back in 2009, Ben Bernanke, then the chairman of the Federal Reserve, was tasked with restoring order to the world's economy in the wake of a mortgage crisis. The main lever he pulled was a timeless one: give large banks more money.

When asked in an interview where this money was coming from — because surely it doesn't just appear out of thin air — he gave a remarkably candid answer.

"To lend to a bank," he explained, "we simply use the computer to mark up the size of the account that they have with the Fed."

It was as though he'd lowered his guard for a moment to state the truth: *Money isn't real. It's just a number we can change in a computer.*

The interviewer seemed momentarily confused by this rare moment of candor, and posed a follow-up question to clarify.

"You've been printing money?" he asked.

"Well, effectively," replied Bernanke.

A few years later, a blogger named Gabrielle Blair (popularly known as @designmom) posted the following message on Twitter: *A Venmo employee could write a line of code that adds $10,000 to every Venmo account, and magically more money would then exist.*

The comment was part of a larger argument, but of the hundreds of people who replied, no one could say why this proposal wouldn't work. Why *can't* a payment service—or a bank, for that matter—decide that its users have $10,000 more today than they did yesterday?

———

Money has always been a product of collective imagination. Throughout history, hype and speculation have produced "bubbles" around questionable markets in everything from Dutch tulips to war bonds to Charles Ponzi's postal coupons. In retrospect, these examples seem exceptional in every sense—mere blips in a story of long-term stability.

But events that were once outliers are now popping up all the time.

Hundreds of people became "Tesla millionaires" when the company's stock rose 700 percent, defying the predictions of just about every professional analyst. Zoom, once a tiny company with a single videoconferencing product that didn't work very well, would suddenly grow to be worth more than every US airline combined.

Meanwhile, shares of AMC Entertainment Holdings, whose core business was movie theaters, surged during a year *in which no one could go to the movies*. Later, the CEO would discover that when he didn't wear pants during an investor call, the stock price would climb higher—thus raising an interesting question of shareholder responsibility: if executives are charged with serving investors to the best of their ability, would no-pants Zoom calls become the new standard for earnings calls across the land?

Even ancient brands like RadioShack, once mocked in *The Onion* with a story about its CEO wondering how his own company could possibly still be in business, experienced bizarre corporate resurrections. At the height of the pandemic, the twice-bankrupt company was purchased for an undisclosed but almost certainly large sum by a couple of crypto bros.*

Simply put, if enough people decide that something is "worth" much more than its current value, then all of a sudden, it is.

I could have written a whole book about the many different points in history when vast sums of money have been created out of nothing—or instantly destroyed as the winds of public opinion change direction.

But the fact that money is based more on perception than objective reality is just our starting point; it's what has allowed the rules of making money to be upended, in unprecedented and revolutionary ways. The goal of this book is to help you

---

* One was an influencer named Tai Lopez, whose Beverly Hills mansion I once visited to film an interview. There was a koi pond running through the living room. A basketball court took up part of the backyard. At the midpoint of the interview, a woman walked through the set wearing a thong bikini, for no obvious reason.

understand how the rules of this game have shifted, and ultimately to answer the question: How can you *win*?

The Money Revolution
(aka Times Change, Smart People Adapt)

Throughout history, a number of broad, important shifts have irreversibly transformed societies and economies. You probably learned about them at some point in school: *the agrarian revolution, the Industrial Revolution,* etc.

Before the Industrial Revolution came along, people worked on their farms and made everything they needed by hand. It was all pretty inefficient, but better than hunting and gathering.

But then! Machinery entered the world, the path to prosperity changed, and large swaths of humanity begin living very differently than their ancestors had. What one's parents and grandparents had done to provide for themselves and their families was no longer the best course for the new generation. To succeed in the Industrial Age, an enterprising peasant had to learn new skills. Sure, some continued doing things the old way, but these were not the ones who thrived.

And so it goes through the ages. Empires rise and fall. Change is constant. Those who adapt are those who prosper.

Today, we stand in the midst of another transformation: the

Money Revolution. Simply put, money ain't what it used to be. This is partly due to the rise of digital assets, but that's only one part of the story. In fact, the *more interesting* parts are the societal and technological shifts creating new paths to prosperity that simply weren't possible—or even imaginable—just a few years ago.

Lurking behind this seismic shift are two parallel trends. The first is a growing distrust of traditional institutions, especially among Gen Zers and millennials, who are on to the fact that the career security their parents and grandparents enjoyed is a thing of the past. Even adjusting for inflation, millennials have paid far more for a college education than any other generation, all while the market value of a degree in most fields has declined. Long-held adages about careers, personal finance, and investing passed on from older generations are increasingly disconnected from their lives.

Confronted with these facts, many young people feel skeptical and resentful of the systems they have inherited. Why shouldn't they? It's a perfectly logical reaction. Besides, revolutions have a habit of showing up when enough people get pissed off. And this time, the revolution is armed with modern tools and methods that greatly amplify its effects.

That's why the second trend is about a growing number of people who are seeking out creative ways to beat the system. Today's winners aren't parking their savings in a comfy 401(k) and waiting for their nest egg to grow, they're putting their cash in alternative investments. They aren't lobbying for legislative action to rein in Wall Street; they're sticking it to hedge funds by squeezing them out of their short positions. They aren't trying to "beat the house" at the casino; they're going on Reddit to learn about prediction markets.

That's because they have decided that the old rules of money—the ones built on trust and a sense of good faith in institutions—aren't just outdated: *the old rules are a scam.*

To be clear, there are real losers in revolutions, too. Just ask Marie Antoinette. Or the followers of Ned Ludd—aka the original Luddites—who rebelled against industrialization by breaking textile machinery (spoiler alert: it didn't work, and they got left behind).

Still, that's the nature of progress. It's not perfect, but with each revolution come new opportunities for more people to share in the wealth.

Money printer go brrrrr.

What Lies Ahead

Before I began writing this book, I undertook a series of experiments. The experiments began as strictly research, but at some point, I kept going. I won't lie: it was fun and addictive.

I bet on the outcome of political elections, learning under

the tutelage of pros. I bet on other markets as well, including the outcome of the Britney Spears conservatorship saga and the state of relations between Kanye West and the Kardashians.

I began playing video games for real money, fulfilling the lifelong dream of my twenty-year-old self.

I learned how to create AI art, focusing my efforts on drawings of cats drinking milkshakes (to view one of my early masterpieces, see page 116).

And of course, I bought meme stocks, because who didn't?

As you'll see, some of these experiments went better than others. At one point I was earning $1,000 a day from something called yield farming. Surely my retirement in Monaco was just a few months away! But while I was watching the numbers go up, the price of the underlying security dropped more than 40 percent.

Then there was the time I made a disastrous mistake and transferred several thousand dollars to the wrong blockchain account. Guess what? When you do that, you can't get it back!

Still, I kept going. All in the name of research, and possibly compulsion.

I went to Denver to see the founder of Ethereum and thousands of his enthusiastic acolytes. I went to Iowa to witness a food cannon that shot vegetables into the sky. I met and interviewed full-time sports bettors, TikTok influencers, professional dungeon masters, and at least one billionaire.

I tried to meet as many people on the front lines of this revolution as I could, in order to tell the best possible story.

Over the course of the next 241 pages, I'll introduce you to some of these enterprising individuals. Among others, you'll meet:

- The skilled programmer who works two full-time jobs simultaneously, without either employer knowing about the other. This isn't a retail worker earning low wages who has to work multiple jobs to make ends meet. Cumulatively, his two jobs pay him over $340,000 a year.
- The TikTok star earning up to $100,000 *a day* selling courses on the decidedly unsexy topic of how to use Microsoft Excel, and another one who gets paid $50,000 a month to sleep through flashing disco lights, techno music played at high volume, and fake FBI raids.
- The British teenager who started a service naming Chinese babies and went on to earn $400,000.
- The game designer who took home first prize in an art fair, for a work "painted" entirely by AI.
- The grandmother who exposed a leading maker of inkjet printers for scamming customers into buying their overpriced name-brand ink cartridges, and won a $1.5-million class-action lawsuit in the process.

And, as they say, so much more.

How to Read This Book

This book is a field guide to the Money Revolution. While it might not always seem this way, even revolutions have rules— or at least, the successful ones do. A revolution without rules is just a riot. So in the pages ahead, you'll learn how to use the new tools and platforms that technology has enabled to capitalize on the new rules of money and gain an advantage for yourself.

Some of the strategies in the pages ahead will be useful to anyone, anywhere, regardless of how much money they currently have access to. Others will be more helpful to those who have some money to invest and are looking for creative ways to make it grow (or simply protect it from loss).

To get the most out of the chapters that follow, it pays to keep the following in mind.

1. Because things change so quickly in times of revolution, some examples you'll read about may no longer be relevant, or may simply be less useful. In those cases, *focus on what you can learn from the story.* Where did the idea come from, and what action did someone need to take to make it happen? Consider how to apply a similar approach to other ideas.

2. Don't be afraid to change your mind. What worked before isn't guaranteed to work now, and what works now won't always work in the future.

3. Most of all, take the advice that makes sense to you and ignore the rest. In fact, that's a good way to read any book.

The stories I'll share are interesting on their own, but I also hope you'll learn something from them. By the time you've finished reading this book, you'll be acquainted with a broad range of strategies to put you on the path to a success story of your own. For example, you'll learn to:

- Get funding from nontraditional markets, including money directly from investors who want to bet on your future.

- Capitalize on asymmetrical opportunities, where the risk is low and the potential reward is high.

- Turn a skill or area of knowledge you already have into a monetizable product that can diversify your income.

- Use simple AI tools to jump-start a creative process or just generate more creative work in a shorter period of time.

- Adopt a new way of thinking that can serve you long into the future as the rules evolve and new opportunities arrive.

This last skill is the most important. As you know by now, the global economy is changing all the time, at a rapid pace.

That's okay, though. Change is constant, but if you understand what brought us to this point and how you can apply these lessons, you'll be way ahead of most people.

To understand why this matters, let's start with one of the core features of this era. In the world of Gonzo Capitalism, everything is for sale.

Chapter Two

Welcome to Peak Marketplace

CONCEPT: The Money Revolution brought us to a stage in modern society in which everything is for sale. Every skill, talent, hobby, or source of knowledge can be monetized. Decentralized platforms allow you to go to market immediately, without banks or other gatekeepers.

There's nothing like massive economic shock to spark a revolution. And the shock precipitated by the pandemic was accompanied by social upheaval just as consequential. Among the most jarring indicators that things were changing, perhaps permanently, was the realization that no matter how advanced our civilization had become, a nasty virus could still show up one day and shut down much of the world.

Whether you lost loved ones, got sick yourself, or somehow escaped the whole thing, chances are you did some reflecting during this period. Everyone did.

It was around this time that millions of people began to question their workplace loyalties. There are many theories about why the Great Resignation happened when it did, but to anyone who was paying attention, it sure seemed like most of these people were quitting simply because they were fed up.

Millions more staged a similar protest in the form of "quiet quitting," a movement that encouraged employees to keep showing up to work and collecting their paychecks but stop working so hard for their employers. Going above and beyond was *so* last year. Even more radical was the *antiwork* subculture that thrived on Reddit. This philosophy borrowed from Marxism to claim that today's model of work, and maybe even capitalism itself, was fundamentally flawed and in need of being dismantled.

All of these movements had two things in common. The first was broad skepticism and distrust of "the system." Corporations and their greedy executives were exploiting workers. The government, regardless of who was in charge, was ineffective. Banks were out to pillage. Wall Street, hedge funds, the revolving door of government and private industry—they were all rigged in favor of elites.

This was the rare social movement that transcended politics. Whether they watched Rachel Maddow or listened to Joe Rogan, the consumers of punditry were mad.

Populism fueled political campaigns, from Bernie Sanders to Donald Trump. Though they were ideological opposites, these elderly New Yorkers skillfully deployed an outsider, antiestablishment message to attract many of the same young and disaffected voters.

The second thing these movements had in common is where things get *complicated*. Many of the self-proclaimed anticapitalists were motivated by money!

Yet another meme, *get the bag*—that is, the bag of money—took hold. The antiworkers didn't like the idea of their employers getting rich on the backs of their low-paid labor, but they weren't philosophically opposed to the idea of acquiring large sums of money themselves. They were mad, sure, but that didn't mean they wanted to live in poverty.

Podcasts were launched with millions of dollars in sponsorship. Instagram influencers hawked handbags and vape pens. More than a million people set up Shopify stores, selling anything you could imagine. At the end of the day, all those people pursuing the work-free life still had to pay their rent.

These realities coexisted, sometimes messily, always in flux.

When One Cargo Door Closes

When school was abruptly canceled in the spring of 2020, social studies teacher Rebecca Rogers went home and began an all-new career.

As the lockdowns and the long hours of virtual teaching stretched on, she found herself increasingly in need of an outlet for burnout and stress. Plus, she liked to experiment. So on a whim, Rogers decided to make an account on TikTok and post videos "making a fool" of herself. A typical video shares a story of something funny or terrible (or both) that happened that day. She also answers questions in a series called *Am I the bad apple?*, a gentler version of Reddit's *Am I the asshole?* forum. Rogers role-plays as multiple characters, frequently splitting between teacher and student perspective, sometimes throwing in an angry parent or power-tripping principal as well.

Her preteen and teenage students were worried that she'd get canceled, but something else happened: she got famous.

And here's where we can begin to see how hardship for some created opportunities for others.

On the heels of lockdowns came the global supply chain crisis. In Britain, a twenty-two-year-old named Jake Slinn started a business buying unopened shipping containers that were backlogged in ports worldwide, then reselling their contents.

Each one he purchased was a grab bag of surprises, like you might see on *Storage Wars*, only these were massive containers holding goods from all over the world. One shipment might contain raw building materials, another one cheap, mass-produced electronics. Artwork, electric scooters, vehicles, French cheese — Jake saw (and resold) it all.

When one cargo door closes, a container ship opens. The disruption in shipping enabled Jake's business to thrive.

Another disruption that spawned a whole new ecosystem of

businesses was the transition to remote work. Companies that had previously resisted allowing their employees to work from home suddenly had no choice—and after some growing pains, the transition turned out to be easier than expected.

Seemingly anything could be moved online, from religious services to therapy to music lessons to a whole host of other activities that had seemed impossible in a remote setting just a few months before. The convenience and scale that this enabled quickly paved the way for all kinds of new business opportunities.

A friend of mine started a virtual mediation group, charging $20 a month. She soon had several thousand dollars in monthly billing and a waiting list. I heard from a dog trainer who offered lessons by Zoom. Legal hearings, doctors' visits, speed dating, you name it…everything was remote, or at least it *could* be.

How It Started, How It's Going

Welcome to the era of "peak marketplace," where everything you can imagine (and many things you can't) can be bought and sold in fast-moving virtual markets.

New networks and forms of payment emerged to serve this new landscape, where anyone selling virtual dog training sessions or the contents of shipping containers could bypass credit card transaction fees and accept payments directly.

Simultaneously, many regulations and controls went out the

window, eliminating the barriers to entry for anyone with an internet connection and an idea. Financial products and models that were once available only to professional traders became widely accessible (for better or worse!).

Even governments realized they could get away with selling just about anything. For a nonrefundable contribution of $150,000, the island nation of Grenada offered citizenship for sale. Not to be outdone, its neighbor Dominica invited you into the family for merely $100,000.

In the US, Yellowstone National Park offered an annual pass for $1,500. Sounds like a good deal for a frequent visitor, but there was just one small catch. The pass (appropriately named the Inheritance Pass) wouldn't be valid *for another 150 years.*

That's right, should the planet still exist in 2172—and assuming the National Park Service is still running the show at Yellowstone—your descendants will be able to visit for free. What a deal!

At the same time, it became easier than ever to accumulate massive numbers of social media followers, monetizing them with ads and brand sponsorships. Countless microcommunities emerged, along with new ways to communicate and create that simply didn't exist before.

Yes, people have been able to "build a social following" since the prehistoric days of MySpace. But not like now.

Rebecca Rogers, the teacher-turned-TikTok-star, amassed more than a million followers in a matter of months. Soon she was flooded with sponsor inquiries and was waking up every day to another 10,000 people tuning in. The direct payment she received for her viral videos paled in comparison to what she earned from partnerships—just like pro athletes with promo deals that vastly eclipse their large contracts to play a sport.

Compare this story to another one I told on my podcast a couple of years ago. In that earlier story, a hardworking teacher had dutifully compiled a collection of foreign-language curriculum aids that she sold online to other teachers, and she went on to make an extra $3,000 a month from her efforts—more than half of her salary from teaching. But in this new era, Rebecca Rogers could make much more than that *from a single sponsored post*. The difference was striking. Not only was her project far more lucrative, it operated on a different scale of engagement.

In this brave new world, *everyone* can be a creator, and the creators (sometimes called influencers, though they aren't the same thing) have all the power. They aren't afraid to use it, either. Collective action campaigns can redistribute wealth, bestow instant celebrity status, or simply wreak havoc on markets.

It's an exciting, confusing, disorienting, and fascinating time to be alive.

Do I Look Sexy in This Electric Car?

The Naked Brand Group (or as its shareholders know it, NAKD) was originally known for its stewardship of

Frederick's of Hollywood, a down-market lingerie brand that operated stores in dying malls across America.* Once the explosion of e-commerce dealt many of these malls a final death blow, Naked Brand turned into a largely online retailer.

Buy hey, so far, so normal: A racy clothing manufacturer struggles to survive in the wake of the near extinction of shopping malls. That's the story?

Here's what's less normal: buoyed by the "anything is possible" era, NAKD made a nakedly ambitious move — they decided to move into a new product line: *electric cars.*

That's right, from lingerie to electric vehicles. It was as though the company's leadership took a look around and said, "Hey guys, what's the hottest thing right now?"

"Well, Tesla is on a tear…"

"Great, let's do what they did!"

So, despite the pesky detail of electric cars having absolutely nothing to do with their existing business, NAKD then pursued a $1.3-billion merger with Cenntro Electric Group, a Chinese EV manufacturer.

Surely such an absurd move would garner nothing more than a laugh, right?

---

* The company's provenance is a little murky. It was founded in Canada, then relocated to New Zealand — all while trading on the (US) NASDAQ stock exchange under the ticker symbol NAKD.

Wrong. Investors pounced, pushing the stock up more than 80 percent. The company now sells fewer fishnets and more smart cars.

In the age of Gonzo Capitalism, nothing is off-limits — even in a bare market.

What Early E-commerce Was Like

To some readers, this next section will sound like someone from the Greatest Generation recounting tales of liberating Europe during World War II. Really, though, this is what it was like. I was on the beach for the main invasion.

All of a sudden, at the turn of the century (2000!), you could sell things online to people wherever they were. EBay, Etsy, and many other marketplaces enabled people to become semiprofessional merchants. As a seller, you could literally walk into stores like Walmart or Toys"R"Us, buy items off the shelves, and then list them online for sale at much more than you paid. (I did this regularly.)

Buyers were extremely trusting or highly suspicious, and sometimes both at the same time. Some buyers thought that anything sold online *surely had to be* an incredible deal; others were equally convinced that everything was a scam. They demanded verification phone calls before making payment for a $10 item.

They asked you to ship their order before they paid. They got mad and left bad reviews if it didn't arrive within two days—long before Amazon made fast shipping an industry standard.

Speaking of payment, buyers sent personal checks or even cash in the mail, sometimes in foreign currency if they were outside the country. I rented a mailbox and stopped by every afternoon to pick up incoming checks and send out the latest packages. Once, a postal clerk asked if she could meet me on her lunch break. It wasn't a date—she just wanted to learn how to start selling online.

From time to time back then, your PayPal account would get shut down for no reason that you could determine. You'd get a generic email saying your account was now closed. That was it: *closed*. Gone. Inaccessible. No appeal was possible, and you couldn't reach anyone at the company to discuss it.

When that happened, you lost whatever funds were in the account—but you weren't fully cut off from the system, which meant you could simply open a new account using the same information. No one at the company cared, or at least no one cared to check.

While selling imported coffee for a season, I proactively registered a second account to protect myself from the whims of PayPal. This account sold the same product, but I registered it using a different business name and made separate auction listings for the coffee.

I soon discovered that the second account had another benefit:

I'd essentially created my own competitor, one that ultimately funneled sales to the same source.

I got a laugh one day when I'd fallen behind on customer support and a buyer messaged me to complain. "I'm going to buy from King Java instead of you," he told me.

King Java, of course, was also me.

It was the best of times, and also the strangest—or so it seemed. Back then I thought that was the time of peak. But it turned out not to be peak at all—it was just *new*. The apex was still to come.

E-commerce Was Fast But Limiting

What we saw then was that these systems opened doors for many people, but not everyone.

"When it comes to selling online," I once said, "no one cares if you're a kid." That was true, to a degree. But most kids running online businesses had help somewhere along the way. They couldn't get their own credit cards or take payments from strangers without an adult somewhere vouching for them.

And it wasn't just kids: small entrepreneurs like me weren't really in control. We still depended on centralized platforms to let us post items for sale, and on big companies to process transactions.

To accept credit cards, for example, we had to get a merchant account from a bank. This was often a challenge, especially for internet retailers trying to explain their business model to old-school bank reps. If you made "too much money," the bank would get suspicious and hold on to your funds. As noted, even PayPal was notoriously bad about this (and still is).

This presented the possibility of a small business owner being squeezed to the breaking point. If you'd taken in a lot of money from a sale and urgently needed it for something—to produce an event that attendees had bought tickets for, for example, or to manufacture the product they'd purchased during a presale— you were out of luck.

Banks didn't care that you'd made sales and had customers waiting. Customers didn't want to hear about your merchant account issues; they just wanted to get what they'd paid for.

TLDR: in this age of e-commerce, banks and centralized platforms had a lot of control. They allowed you to run your business, but they also had the power to shut you down.

Fast, Weird, and Decentralized

I've been part of the online business world for twenty-five years, and I've been writing stories about the "new economy" for almost as long. As I researched this book and talked with people, I sensed that something was different this time—but what was it, exactly? What is it about the postpandemic economy that makes it so distinct?

I finally settled on three qualities: *fast, weird,* and *decentralized.* Most of the stories you'll read in this book fit at least one of those descriptions, and often more than one. Moreover, the qualities tend to reinforce one another. When something is fast and decentralized, for example, it tends to achieve massive early growth—and it's also likely to be something you've never heard of before.

Faster than ever

The speed and scale of today's business models are much different from the olden days, circa the early 2010s.

MrBeast, one of the most popular YouTubers of all time, earned *tens of millions* of dollars before his twenty-third birthday. He also once picked up 159,000 new followers *in a single day.* When he wanted to expand his reach further, he simply dubbed his videos into Spanish. It wasn't long before his Spanish-language channel had grown from 300,000 viewers to 22 million, *in a single year.**

Further translations into Hindi and Portuguese soon followed, as did another influx of new subscribers. (MrBeast does not actually speak any of these languages, and no one seems to care.)

---

* https://www.dailymail.co.uk/femail/article-11429671/MrBeast-followed-person
-YouTube.html.

In the cryptocurrency world, newly launched coins could attract huge sums of money from investors. Sometimes the investors didn't know anything about the project! "It sounds cool" was a good-enough justification. Besides, time was of the essence. If you waited for verification or some attempt at due diligence, you might be too late.

Weirder than ever

For the better part of a century, the way workers prepared to enter and advance in the workforce was somewhat predictable. You completed a certain amount of higher education, obtaining degrees or certificates or other expensive markers of approval.

You crafted your résumé, went on lots of interviews, and amassed LinkedIn recommendations. At a certain point, some employer would invite you to join their tribe, or perhaps their multinational corporation. In exchange for a certain number of weekly hours, and some labor (presumably, but not necessarily) related to the education you'd undertaken, you'd receive the agreed-upon compensation. In the process, you'd deposit your paycheck into a few different accounts, including one for your daily expenses and one that you used to save for the future. You chose from a selection of retirement plans and dutifully tried to contribute over time. Hopefully your employer chipped in something as well.

Mostly, you crossed your fingers that it would be enough

money to live on at some point in the faraway future. In the meantime, you tried to manage more immediate issues: housing, loans, and so on.

There were, of course, alternatives to both these paths. Some people opted out of traditional employment and started a business. Others invested more aggressively or didn't invest at all. And *every once in a while* you'd meet someone who was making a living in a way that felt truly radical.

Again, I've been studying unusual businesses for a long time. In a previous book, *Side Hustle,* I wrote about a guy who drop-shipped live crickets to reptile owners. I once covered a story about a start-up called BirdSupplies.com, which specialized in "anti–feather plucking" products for parrots. I've interviewed a professional Hula-Hoop instructor, an engineer-turned-professional-snuggler, and even a guy who ate nothing but potatoes for a year — before becoming a diet and fitness coach.

It takes a lot to surprise me, in other words.

But as bizarrely creative as some of those business ventures were, even I've been astonished by the sheer ingenuity of all the weird stuff being bought and sold today. In the UK, a twenty-seven-year-old put his imaginary friend up for sale on eBay, saying he'd outgrown the relationship. It attracted a dozen bids.

In San Francisco, a group of entrepreneurs opened a pop-up rat café, where visitors can sip their coffee while cozying up to live, free-roaming rats. (One online commenter quipped: "I'm from Brooklyn, we don't have to pay extra for that.")

The list goes on and on. If weird was already the new normal back when I started writing and podcasting about side hustles, over the last few years I've nevertheless found plenty of examples that out-weirded the old ways.

This is by design. In the era of peak marketplace, the more novel your offerings, the more likely they are to stand out and get attention. In this crowded, noisy marketplace of goods and ideas, novelty and creativity are currency.

Or put another way: Weird sells.

Decentralized (for the first time)

In Goa, India, a financial entrepreneur launched a one-stop money management ecosystem that attracted $7 million in capital, including an investment from Mark Cuban. Inspired by a workshop he had attended a year before, its founder had taught himself coding and racked up a few months of consulting experience before sitting down to build his decentralized investing platform—which he did in his spare time, when he wasn't attending middle school.

This financial entrepreneur—Gajesh Naik, age thirteen—may well represent the peak example of peak marketplace. There have always been smart, precocious kids who are good at computers and math. And hackers are often young. But how often does a preteenager in India pull in millions of dollars of investment capital in a matter of months?

On decentralized platforms, it's not so much that no one cares if you're a kid—it's that no one even knows if you're a kid. That's because decentralized networks allow services to operate in a "trustless" system where everything is publicly visible—except for the identities of the wizard or wizards behind the curtain, and sometimes even the participants themselves.

The term *decentralized* used to refer to the darkest, most nefarious corners of the web: places like Silk Road, the marketplace that operated as a Walmart for aspiring anarchists, where all kinds of forbidden goods were available for sale. If you wanted to buy a grab bag of synthetic drugs, or maybe a grenade launcher, and have it shipped to your home by FedEx, Silk Road was the place to go.

Of course, decentralized platforms that sell nefarious products still exist. But so do countless legitimate platforms that traffic in more typical activity. In the parlance of Gonzo Capitalism, *decentralized* doesn't necessarily mean "shady"—it just means "open to everyone." It's a principle of internet architecture, where power is distributed away from banks and other institutions and into the hands of "the community."

At least in theory. As you'll see, the concept is problematic and far from perfect in its current versions. Sometimes it's more of an aspiration or ideal than a reality. Instead of being a free-to-everyone trading zone, for example, Silk Road was actually more like a commercial business run by a lone kingpin, who is now living out his years on a double life sentence in a supermax prison.

It also had some other problems that went beyond the fact that you could order heroin and flamethrowers to your door. For one thing, Bitcoin payments are "virtually untraceable" in theory, but in practice, all it takes is a single mistake somewhere in your chain of transactions for authorities to find you. After the Silk Road infrastructure was taken down, federal agents from a dozen countries went on a spree of arresting hundreds of customers who thought their anonymity was protected.

Nevertheless, the concept of power being *less centralized,* if not fully unleashed from a central authority, features in many of the stories you'll read in the pages ahead.

It Sounds Strange, But It's (Usually) Rational

The various moneymaking ideas you'll read about in this book are truly eccentric, to the point where you might wonder how they can possibly be successful. Yet most of them are grounded in time-tested business principles. Even the products or services that may sound absurd at first usually meet a few simple requirements common to most successful markets. For example:

Supply and demand: At the University of California, Berkeley, enrollment is capped for some of the most popular classes — so an ambitious student set up a way to bid on his unwanted slots. If you want to get into a course and it's full, why wouldn't you use a marketplace that connects buyers and sellers?

Limited space or other constraints: In Japan, one enterprising individual developed a service that lets fellow office workers in search of peace and quiet use car-sharing platforms to rent cars *without ever driving them anywhere*. It may sound crazy, but Tokyo is a crowded place, and renting a car in a parking garage for a quiet lunch or an hour of privacy makes sense.

Geographic or economic advantage: The dental capital of the world is Los Algodones, Mexico, a border town just fifteen minutes from Yuma, Arizona. It's also known as Molar City, since the small area includes more than 350 dental clinics, set up for the express purpose of providing affordable services to visiting Americans, who cross the border to save up to 70 percent on implants, crowns, and other common procedures.

The dentists in Los Algodones are able to offer such savings not only because most dental materials and equipment are generally cheaper in Mexico. It's also because many industries, including dental practitioners, create artificial scarcity and engage in price-fixing. In other words, dental work in the US is more expensive than it needs to be, because the industry colludes to keep prices high.

Operating in a nearby jurisdiction (or even a faraway one) that isn't subject to as many constraints allows you to offer lower prices to those willing to visit—while still making a profit.

Appealing to nostalgia and shared values: A record label in Indiana has been issuing music releases in deliberately obscure formats as part of a protest against streaming services where every track is available on demand. Recent formats have included cassettes covered in shards of broken glass and an entire album on a length of unspooled magnetic tape.

The fact that you can't actually listen to some of the music by this record label is considered a *benefit* to people who are nostalgic for the days of tape decks and vinyl. (If that doesn't make sense to you, you're not the target market.)

Desperation: If you happened to buy hundreds of Bitcoins at a bargain price a decade ago, but then forgot the password to your wallet (sadly, a common problem), you can hire a "Bitcoin Recovering Hypnotist" to jog your memory.

You see why this is an efficient market, right? If you lost that password and a hypnotist could actually help, it would be worth whatever it cost.

In other words, as strange as it all seems, there's some rationality to most of these things — at least most of the time.

What's in It for You?

Make no mistake, this is a confusing and disorienting time. It would be easy to write it off as irrational exuberance, as many people have.

But fortune favors the prepared, and good things come to those who take action. When I last talked to Rebecca Rogers, the social studies teacher turned TikTokker, she had started a podcast—which had subsequently been purchased by a big production company. She was also scheduled to speak at eight educational conferences over the next few months.

Making funny teacher videos turned out to be so much more than just a quick viral hit, soon to be forgotten. Those videos led Rebecca into a new career with seemingly unlimited potential.

Pundits have prematurely predicted the arrival of peak marketplace before. It was easy to do. After all, the proliferation of markets is a natural by-product of progress and economic growth.

But until now, this growth had limits. It was like the rental car with a speedometer cap that I had once in Dubai. Whenever I got a few miles above the legal speed limit, it started beeping at me and wouldn't stop until I slowed down. If I tried to push it further, it simply wouldn't accelerate at all.

Today, the speedometer cap is gone. Everyone has some talent they can monetize, some service they can offer, some idea they can sell.

There's a new marketplace; it's called Everywhere.

And if you want to be part of it—pay attention. If everyone else is "getting the bag," where's yours?

Chapter Three

Bet on Britney

CONCEPT: You can now bet real money on election outcomes, international events, the economy, and anything else you can imagine—including Britney Spears. If you'd like to start your own betting market, you can do that, too. For the best odds of success, ignore your personal views and look for mispriced markets.

Quick, who's going to be the next US president? What about the next Supreme Court justice? And will the latest climate bill ever make it through Congress?

If you live in America (or pay attention to what goes on in America), no doubt you have opinions on these questions. You also know that these opinions are divisive. But here's something new: you can now bet *real money* on them. If you feel like you have insight into what's going to happen in the next election cycle—or any number of other future events—you can profit from your predictions.

Experiments in Amateur Punditry

When I learned about betting on prediction markets, I thought I'd study up on it as research for this book. I would read the academic literature, interview experts, and dispassionately write about the experience.

Who am I kidding? I'm competitive and compulsive. Naturally, I imagined I'd be good enough to make money with it.

For my first foray into the world of prediction markets, I turned to PredictIt.org, one of the earliest political betting markets to operate at scale. A "market" is essentially a betting pool, and there are a couple of hundred markets open at any given time, allowing people to bet real money on all sorts of political events.

A few typical examples:

- The president's approval rating
- How many votes the chair of the Federal Reserve will receive
- Which party will win the Arizona senate race
- The next G20 leader to leave office

I made an initial deposit of $1,000, then started placing bets. The 2022 midterms were a full year and a half away, but I was already sure there was no way Marco Rubio would lose Florida, and that House Democrats were almost certain to lose seats. Would another Supreme Court justice be up for confirmation hearings in the next three months? *Hmmm. Let me check with my sources.*

The market predicted only 20 percent odds for the last question, but I took the bet and put down $100.

For two weeks, I actively monitored the site, seeking out new markets to bet on, and swings in opinion. I scored a major win when I was browsing via desktop computer and received a news alert on my phone: *Netanyahu to step down as Israel's long-serving prime minister.*

I quickly clicked over to a betting market on "Israel's next prime minister" and put down $100 on the runner-up, who had been lagging in the polls behind Netanyahu.

Within a minute or two, the odds changed, but not before I'd placed my bet. Two weeks later, when the transfer of power was official, I collected $60 in winnings, along with the return of my original $100.

That's when I realized that making real money in these markets isn't just about making an educated guess and then sitting back to see what happens—it's also about monitoring news and trends and acting quickly on what you learn. After that, I kept PredictIt open in a tab and began paying much closer attention to news alerts. I wasn't usually quick enough to respond the way I'd done that first time, but once in a while I could pull in an easy win.

To be fair, I got a little lucky with my real-time wager on Netanyahu's departure. Most of the time, you aren't going to make quick money just by signing up for news notifications. By going deeper, however, you *can* gain a real advantage. Unlike the stock market, which features huge numbers of traders (including many with access to tools that you and I can't get), prediction markets are still new enough that it's possible for an average yet diligent researcher to come out ahead. Exact numbers are hard to pin down, but the experts I spoke with suggested there are at least a few hundred people earning $50,000 a year or more betting on elections.

Place Your Wager

Weirdly, PredictIt is owned by Victoria University of Wellington—that would be Wellington, *New Zealand*. That's right, for years, one of the few sites where US citizens could legally bet on US elections was run by a university thousands of miles away.

Until recently, this has all been perfectly legit, thanks to a convoluted agreement the university reached with the Commodity Futures Trading Commission (CFTC). To make the CFTC happy, PredictIt had to agree to operate within a series of limitations. The biggest one is money: users can bet up to a maximum of only $850 in every market. Other conditions included a cap on how many users can take part in any particular market (5,000);

that the market would be used only for academic and research purposes; and that it would be run as a nonprofit, without brokerage charges or commissions. (PredictIt also promised to be on good behavior and clean its room before going out to play.)*

A cap of $850 per market might seem limiting, but if you want to bet higher amounts, you just need to spread your money around. Hundreds of markets are open at any particular time, giving you lots of options. Furthermore, there are often multiple markets asking the same question, just in different forms.

For example, both of these markets might be available for betting:

Market 1. Will the Republicans win the House in the
next election?
Yes
No
Market 2. Which party will control the House after the
next election?
Republicans
Democrats

Since the US is effectively a two-party system, these are two opportunities to bet on the same prediction. If you were

---

* As I was in the midst of writing this book, the CFTC decided to ground PredictIt for the foreseeable future. The organization appealed the decision, and the case has been winding its way through the court system.

highly confident in either outcome (Yes/No) of the first market, you could bet up to $850 on that question. Then you could bet another $850 on the second (Republicans/Democrats), doubling your stake. If you were only a little confident, on the other hand, you could bet the full $850 on that outcome in one market and hedge your bet by placing a smaller amount on the opposite outcome in another.

As I began experimenting with various strategies, it became clear that the built-in guardrails can be overridden with some strategic planning. It didn't take long, however, for bad habits to set in. I approached political betting like your average day trader: compulsively, and badly. I became emotionally attached to my bets, and assigned too much meaning to wins and losses. When my bet paid off, I was a genius: Soon I'd be writing for *Foreign Affairs* and appearing on C-SPAN. When I lost, which was more often than not, I felt terrible. *How come I didn't see that committee change coming?* I wondered.

Finally, I decided that if I wanted to learn to be a better bettor, I would have to seek out the experts.

Negative Risk (Where You Actually Can't Lose)

If you're serious about making real money through prediction markets, it helps to learn how to read raw polling data and brush up on your knowledge of probability theory. But I was more interested in learning about a concept known as *negative risk*. This was mind-boggling at first, so I took some time to understand it.

First, a warning: if you Google the phrase *negative risk*, most results will refer to activities such as having unprotected sex, taking drugs of unknown origin, and driving with someone who's been drinking.

Those are very different topics altogether.

In the world of prediction markets, *negative risk* refers to bets that are impossible to lose, because of how a particular market is settled. Betting in negative-risk situations is actually the opposite of risky: your expected value (EV) is positive, so you lose only if you *don't* take the bet.

This remarkable situation tends to occur in markets that offer more than two possible outcomes, like when a lot of people are running for president. These are known as *multiple-contract markets*, and savvy bettors can place bets on lots of different scenarios.

A common example is something like: "Who will be the Republican nominee in 2024?"

Primary elections can be crowded, attracting a dozen or more viable candidates. In addition to the top tier of three or four, a second tier of less-likely candidates fills out the ranks.

Each candidate is its own *yes/no* market, meaning you can place individual bets against all the candidates you think are unlikely to advance. After all, in a primary election there can be only one winner and many losers.

Here's a hypothetical market:

Who will be the Republican nominee in 2024?
-Governor of Sunshine State
-Former vice president
-Reality-TV star
-Senator from Texas
-Congressman no one has heard of
-Guy at the sandwich shop

(The real market could have a dozen or more additional candidates, but we'll stop there.)

Markets are usually composed of outcomes that add up to 100 percent. In other words, in a simple yes/no market where the odds of the "yes" outcome were predicted at 60 percent, the odds of the "no" outcome would be 40 percent.*

In a negative-risk situation, however, the possible outcomes add up to more than 100 percent. This happens because you can bet yes *or* no on multiple candidates. In these situations, arbitrage opportunities can occur.

If it's still confusing, just remember this: negative risk describes

---

* Instead of percentages, many betting sites use a betting scale of $0 to $1. You could buy "yes" shares at 60 cents or sell "no" shares at 40 cents, for example. To learn more about negative risk (it's a little complicated), check out the free guides at predicting politics.com.

a scenario in which, by making multiple bets, *you can make money regardless of the winner.* If you bet against every candidate in a long list, you'll be wrong about one of them—but your gains from being right on all the others will exceed your one big loss.

It's Not Just Politics: Enter Polymarket & Friends

After experimenting with PredictIt for a few weeks, I dove into another platform called Polymarket. This platform allows bets on all sorts of markets, not just political events. Among other things, you could vote on whether Britney Spears would be released from her father's conservatorship, the number of people going through airport security on any given day, whether Kanye West's next album will be streamed more than 100 million times in its first week, and whether a hurricane would make landfall in the lower 48 US states in the next month.

Just for fun, I voted on Britney Spears being released from her conservatorship and won nearly $200. Free Britney!* Then I voted on the number of people passing through TSA security lines daily—I fly a lot, so surely I'm an expert, I reasoned—and promptly lost $100.

---

* I'll admit that only later did I wonder if this was exploitive in some way. Britney doesn't lose anything from this practice, but she also doesn't profit from it, which seems unfair. To be safe, I decided to stick with betting on politicians, who I figured were fair game.

If you think this sounds a lot like gambling, you're right... at least somewhat. In a sense, it *is* a form of gambling, which is why regulators are trying to shut down some of these sites.

But prediction markets serve at least one important purpose that typical sports betting sites do not. By using the prediction data aggregated in these markets, experts can make *their own* predictions about everything from the trajectory of the economy to looming upsets of the existing political order to where the next big snowstorm might hit. In other words, they can be used for legitimate research purposes — so legitimate, in fact, that Harvard Business School offers a course on Forecasting Using Prediction Markets.

And in some cases, this aggregate data is better at predicting future events than experts, polling, or media coverage. That's because, as the "wisdom of the crowds" theory explains, when the predictions of a large and diverse group of nonexperts are combined, they sometimes can be more accurate than the reporting of trained professionals.

Betting markets are also a way for forecasters to look beyond posturing and "Twitter outrage." After all, just because everyone is mad about something doesn't mean it's going to change. When you ask people to put money down on their beliefs, they suddenly become more rational. For one example, consider how these markets out-predicted most professional pundits during a season of political drama in the United Kingdom.

According to hundreds of media articles published in the

spring of 2022, Prime Minister Boris Johnson was going to lose his job. In the preceding months, he'd walked into a series of blunders, most notably enacting strict Covid laws for the nation, then conveniently ignoring them himself.

It was a very British scandal, calling the notion of fairness into question and highlighting the hypocrisy of a leader who said one thing while doing another.

For weeks, it was the lead story in the UK media. Even the conservative tabloids that had backed Johnson for election piled on. They understood how to tap into public sentiment, and that sentiment was outrage.

Many of the articles tried to predict the timing of Johnson's downfall. The consensus seemed to be that he would be pushed out; the only real question was whether he'd survive for days or weeks.

Curious, I checked the betting markets on PredictIt and other sites. By a margin of 9 to 1, Johnson was predicted to hold on! Almost all of the pros and serious politicos believed he'd weather the storm. *Hmmm. What did they know?*

Surprisingly—or not, depending on which view you held— Johnson did indeed hold on to power, at least for several more months through the spring and summer. In this case, the crowd was smarter than the talking heads, most of whom thought the whole affair would lead to his swift downfall.

I bet $100 on Johnson staying put (at least for the time being), and I won. But of course, this wasn't a genius-level bet—the markets had already been priced to reflect the fact that it's hard to topple a prime minister, especially one as wily as Johnson, who had survived several previous scandals.*

Is All This Really Legal?

Well, yes and no. Polymarket operates in a quasi-legal structure of being partly centralized and partly decentralized. After going back and forth with regulators, who argued that businesses that facilitated betting markets couldn't just set up randomly without proper licensing, Polymarket was ultimately forced to close to US investors in 2022. It continued to serve anyone living elsewhere, as well as any US residents who used a virtual private network (VPN) to access the site.

Just as Polymarket and PredictIt were closing up shop (at least to Americans), another project called Kalshi was petitioning lawmakers for permission to open legally for everyone. Like Polymarket, Kalshi also hopes to offer trading in a wide array of markets. You can bet on big elections, sure, but you can also bet on how many people will "like" Elon Musk's next tweet, on the future price of gas, or on what the next virus to cause a pandemic will be.

---

* Johnson was eventually toppled and forced to resign. But not until many months later, and only in response to new developments and a different scandal.

It's hard to predict which platforms that offer prediction markets will end up sticking around and gaining approval to operate widely. But if there's one sure, safe bet, it's that we'll be seeing more and more of these betting markets cropping up in the years ahead. When one virtual trading floor closes, look for another.

Before long you'll be able to download apps that make it easy to get onboarded. Money transfers will be seamless, and there will be no shortage of markets to consider. The bottom line: if it's not possible to bet real money in a nontraditional market now, it will be very soon.

How Not to Lose All Your Money

Predicting politics was fun. The more I played around on different sites, the more I enjoyed the freewheeling, unregulated environment they existed in.

Alas, this is where I made a truly colossal error—one that reminded me that the absence of any central authority overseeing these platforms also comes with a cost.

After I'd gotten set up on one of these betting platforms, I went to transfer several thousand dollars to my digital wallet. I figured it would be simple enough—I'd done it before, and had saved a unique wallet ID in my address book—or so I thought. In reality it turned out that whatever ID I'd saved wasn't the one I was supposed to use in transferring money.

When the funds didn't turn up in my account after a few hours, I wrote to the support team and was relieved when a representative responded promptly and promised to help. *Great*, I thought. *Even if I did something stupid, they can fix it.*

An hour later, however, the rep emailed again with bad news. I'd sent my money to a "burned" wallet–effectively, one that they couldn't access.

"The money's just gone?" I asked, dumbfounded.

"I'm sorry," the rep said. "But yes, that's correct."

I protested a few more times, and each time the support team was responsive and polite. They also confirmed, however, that there was nothing they could do.

If you lose your credit card, you can call the bank and they'll refund any charges after it left your possession. If you overpay a business, the business is usually obligated to refund the overage or apply it to a future payment—and if they don't, as long as you were using a credit or debit card, you can simply call your bank to contest the charge.

That's not how it works on sites like Polymarket. There, payments are decentralized and stored on the blockchain, which means that transactions are strictly between two parties, unmediated by any bank or credit card company. The problem is that what happens on the blockchain stays on the blockchain, quite literally. In other words, transactions are irreversible.

That's the funny thing about an irreversible transaction: it cannot be reversed.

Losing your money to the ether instead of to another person is uniquely depressing. It's the equivalent of lighting cash on fire. When you transfer to the wrong address, not only can you never get it back, no one else can access it either. The money simply ceases to exist, at least for all practical purposes. Good times!

Let my loss be a lesson for you. When you're transacting with real money on decentralized networks, *be careful*. Send small payments first, then confirm that they made it before transferring larger amounts.

GETTING SET UP

Getting set up to play in these markets can be easier or harder depending both on the type of platform and on the regulations that govern who can access it.

For platforms that are truly decentralized, you don't even need to register — you'll just connect your digital wallet. For centralized and partially centralized markets, you'll register and make an account just as with any other site.

For sites that are geo-restricted (that is, available or legal only in certain areas), however, you may need to use a VPN to gain access. Note that some platforms are required to use a KYC system — short for *know your customer* — in which they verify your identity prior to betting. It's harder to sneak through in those situations.

Get Paid for Predicting the Future: A Brief Guide

A project called Polymarket Whales tracks all the large bets made on the platform and posts them publicly, so you can see exactly where people are winning or losing large amounts of money. (These people are identified only through their blockchain wallet addresses—a long string of numbers beginning with *0x*—so you don't know who they are.)

Combing through the entries on the site reveals a lot of interesting patterns. At one point, for example, I noticed that someone had made hundreds of thousands of dollars betting on whether Tom Brady would continue to play in the NFL for another year. Someone else was less lucky and had lost $40,000 on the likelihood of Twitter adding an edit button to its interface. At first these bets seem completely random, but over time you can learn a lot about what it takes to earn (or at least not to lose) money in prediction markets.

The obvious way to profit from prediction markets is to make accurate predictions, but of course that's easier said than done. Remember, a lot of other smart people are trying to do the same thing. Furthermore, the betting odds favor the outcomes that most people expect, meaning that the more likely you are to win any given bet, the lower your winnings will be.

Consider a possible market for the chance of rain tomorrow.

If every weather forecast predicts a 98 percent chance of rain, you won't be able to make money (at least not much) by placing a $100 bet that rain will indeed occur. Very few people would bet against you! Not only that, you'd also have to accept very unfavorable odds, which means you'd be risking a lot to gain a little. After all, there is *some* chance that it won't rain. If it doesn't, you've lost $100. And even if it does rain, you've won only $2.

Let's take a real example. In the run-up to the 2020 election, Joe Biden made news by speculating that he might try to increase the number of Supreme Court justices.

In the wake of his remarks, a number of betting markets popped up to answer the question, "If elected, will Biden pack the Court?"

In a short period of time, the odds became clear: *almost no one thought this would actually happen.* After all, it would be a bold and largely unprecedented move, at least in the context of recent history, and any attempt would surely set off a high-stakes political battle that a new administration could ill afford.

At least according to the betting markets, there was never more than a 1:10 chance of the move succeeding. Most of the time, the odds were even lower.

The markets were right. Biden's flex turned out to be strictly political: his supporters used it to drum up campaign contributions and turnout and fundraising, while his critics did the same with their constituencies. In the end, both sides got back to business and prepared for the next battle. Everyone who took the long odds by betting "yes" ended up compensating all the people who took the other side of the bet.

Granted, if Biden had actually tried—and succeeded—to add an extra justice or two, you could have done very well by choosing those long odds. At 1:20 (95 percent to 5 percent), every $100 you bet would have produced a return of $1,900, minus commissions.

Tempting as this sounds, remember that for every person making money on a bet, many more are losing. And no matter how much of a "sure thing" your prediction might seem, you still need to be careful. After all, the belief that you simply "can't lose" has led to the downfall of countless speculators throughout history.

Instead of betting in a market because you believe your prediction is right, you want to find the one where you believe lots of other people are *wrong*. These *mispriced markets*, the targets of successful traders and card counters the world over, are where the advantages lie.

After three months of regular betting on politics and other assorted events, my own record was mixed. I got a few things right—but I also got a lot wrong. If you're smarter than me and want to give it a try, here's a starting point.

Do your research. Learn as much as you can about the topic you want to put money on. Dig deep, and get in the habit of reviewing primary sources (like poll data) instead of relying on secondary news media. Spend time on networks like Reddit and Discord. Check pinned messages in the forums that answer common questions. YouTube videos may be helpful as well, but be careful about any advice that seems markedly different from what you hear elsewhere. Seek out a beginner's guide on the topic, and try to question your assumptions as you go along.

Ask questions in the forums. When I started posting on Discord, I incorrectly assumed that providing an introduction or some context to my query would be helpful. I quickly learned otherwise: keep it short and specific, and just ask your question.

> ☑ *"Does anyone know when the latest poll numbers will be released?"*
> ☒ *"Hey everyone, hope you're doing well. I was wondering if anyone knows when the latest poll numbers will come out? I was thinking it could be helpful in ..."*

Practice with low-stakes bets. Prediction markets can be a great place to practice because you can make bets for $10 or less. Start with $100 and spread it out across as many bets as possible. Sure, you might lose a lot of them at first, but it's a relatively cheap education. Or, to avoid losses altogether while you're learning the ropes, try using a platform where you can bet with play money in some form.

Put aside your personal views (and ignore the personal views of others). Most betting market pages include a comments section, which should be treated the same way as any comments section on the internet (i.e., ignored). Even in the relatively tame environment of prediction markets, political discourse leaves much to be desired. Don't let yourself be influenced by opinions presented as facts, half-truths, or statements that are flat-out wrong.

Ignoring the fiery debates that often erupt in comment threads will also help you avoid getting swayed by your own beliefs or emotions. Betting on political events isn't about expressing your political preferences. It's about making a judgment about *what you think is actually going to happen.* I found this difficult to do at first, but once real money was at stake, I learned to be apolitical, or at least set my personal views to the side.

Bet on swings. One of the simplest strategies you can adopt is to simply "ride the wave" of volatile markets. Markets that take a long time to resolve, like for a presidential election that may be a year or more away, tend to go up and down in response to events and polls.

Instead of trying to predict the ultimate result — which ties up your money for a long time, even if you're correct — try placing lots of smaller bets on events or milestones that occur along the way. Just be sure to choose an exit point at which you'll take profits or cut your losses. The point is to be quick and get out.

Factor in commissions. Most betting platforms charge fees, which you need to factor into your expected winnings. As the saying goes, the house always wins. PredictIt walks away with

10 percent of every winning bet, and even the platforms that are completely decentralized have some kind of fee structure, because there are real costs involved in maintaining the system.

Capitalize on other people's irrationality. Most people who bet, whether on political events or sports or the messy lives of pop stars, end up becoming emotionally attached to their preferred outcome.

I've already mentioned that you want to avoid this habit for your own wagers, but you can also gain an edge simply by being mindful of how it affects others. This is especially true in big races like presidential elections, high-stakes sporting events like the NFL championship or the World Cup, and all sorts of "culture issues" that are particularly divisive.

Cash in on conspiracy theories. Speaking of emotional betting, capitalizing on mass delusions can be one of the most profitable strategies in political betting.

Take what happened right after the 2020 presidential election, after Joe Biden had clearly won but Donald Trump refused to concede. As more and more evidence came in that reinforced Biden's margin of victory, some Trump supporters simply refused to accept reality and kept doubling down on their bets. Pro betters on PredictIt and Polymarket called this "free MAGA money," meaning it was freely available for the taking.

Look for "99 percent bets." These are bets in which most people agree that the market in question is effectively decided, even though it hasn't yet been settled (closed) by the platform.

This tends to happen when an election result is awaiting mail-in ballots, when a candidate drops out before a winner is formally announced, or in the final seconds of a game where a comeback is all but impossible.

Wagering on 99 percent bets can still be risky, because to profit from the odds you typically have to bet a lot to win a little. That said, these bets are as close to a sure thing as they get. Make a lot of them, and the winnings will eventually add up.

———————

After experimenting for a while, I had a lot of respect for the prediction market pros. I also realized I'd never be one of them. Instead of being truly good, I'd be the kind of person who *thinks* he's good. I might win a few big bets here and there, but those wins would just bring me false confidence—a dangerous quality for aspiring gamblers.

Probability theory not being my strong suit, I'd also get a lot wrong. Then I'd second-guess myself and chase bets I shouldn't just to "catch up." In short, I'd be exactly the kind of person the pros enjoy betting against: someone who thinks they're better than they really are. As the old poker saying goes, if you look around the table and don't see the sucker, you're the sucker.

I didn't want to be the sucker, so in the end I moved on to other things.

Chapter Four

Double Your Paycheck

CONCEPT: "Multiworking" at two or more full-time jobs is not for the faint of heart — but under the right conditions, you can double your income without working twice as much.

It's early in the morning when Jacob H. logs on to a company intranet and begins his workday. His employer is in Connecticut, but Jacob lives in Colorado, where he's two hours behind Eastern Time. He doesn't mind the time difference, though — he's gotten used to different schedules ever since the start of the pandemic, when all employees were sent home to work remotely.

After a few false starts, where workers were called upon to return only to be sent home again after a new wave of infections appeared, the company announced an official policy that coming into the office would forever be optional. Within thirty days,

Jacob had packed a U-Haul and relocated to Boulder, where he spent the weekends biking and hiking.

But today is a weekday, so he dutifully works through a series of IT-related tasks for two hours, at which point he opens up a second laptop and logs on to a different company's network. There, he begins *another* day's work, this one for an engineering company located in the Midwest. For the next eight or so hours, he toggles between both jobs, doing his best to avoid double-booking meetings. He makes sure to participate in each company's internal communication channels throughout the day and send a steady stream of updates to each of his teams.

The extra effort is worth it. Jacob takes home two paychecks — not just a job and a side income, but *two full-time salaries* that add up to more than $340,000 a year. And no one at either job has any idea that he's doubling up.

He told me all about it when we spoke one evening via Zoom (we had to talk at night because, you guessed it, his mornings and afternoons are taken). All that you're about to read is true, except for his name, which I've changed per his request.

If Jacob were working at a physical office with coworkers, it would be extremely difficult, if not impossible, to get away with this secret life. Not just because it would be harder to avoid detection, but because the hours he now spends being hyperproductive would dissolve into meetings, interruptions, and all the distractions that would prevent him from accomplishing two full sets of tasks.

Jacob acknowledges that having two jobs can sometimes be its own source of distraction, though he says it helps that one of the jobs is a little less traditional, with a CEO who's absent a lot. Plus, he said, working remotely saves him so much time that he's able to effectively fit two workdays into one.

Working *two full-time jobs during overlapping hours* without either employer being aware of the other might sound a bit radical. But Jacob is not alone. Whether by choice, necessity, or happy accident, a burgeoning subset of professionals have found a clever way to hack the system by working multiple jobs at the same time.

These aren't college students stringing together retail jobs to earn money for books and pizza, or even entry-level employees working in under-the-radar administrative roles. More often, they're experienced professionals: coders, system administrators, engineers, accountants, and skilled knowledge workers of all kinds. Many of them earn a six-figure salary from each employer.

Some of them do it as an act of protest ("All employment is time theft," as another person I spoke with put it). Many others do it for the cash. And some may simply do it for the constant stimulation it provides. "It's like a video game," Jacob said. "Just with higher stakes."

It can be stressful and demanding, and it isn't for everyone. But some people thrive under this kind of pressure. It also comes with an obvious reward: earning twice as much money as before.

Multiworking: Work (Multiple Jobs) from Anywhere

It's hard to find precise estimates of how common this practice is—people being paid for multiple jobs at the same time are understandably protective of their secret—but it's more common than you'd think, and not difficult to see why.

The rise of multiworking can be explained in two words: *remote work*. The pandemic made the practice of work-from-anywhere commonplace, forcing employers that had previously refused to allow employees to work independently to suddenly update their policies. In some cases, it turned out that remote work was preferable for these companies: The change allowed them to save on rent and utilities, and it even led to greater productivity.

Once that door was opened, it was hard to shut. At many companies, remote work quickly became the norm, not a perk afforded to a small number of high-performing employees. While some eventually returned to policies that required office attendance, plenty of others now let the majority of their employees work from home at least two or three days a week, and some allow workers to remain fully remote.

"But isn't he cheating his bosses . . . ??"

If you happen to be an executive or manager, you might be reading this with alarm.

Even if you aren't in a leadership role, you might be thinking, *These people are cheating their employers! With their attention split between bosses, surely they can't be doing a good job for either one!* You might even wonder if it's legal to secretly work two jobs at the same time.

I mean, sure, it's a little sneaky. But until job contracts start explicitly stating that workers can't be employed elsewhere simultaneously, it's hard to pinpoint exactly what infraction is being committed (provided there isn't some obvious conflict of interest).

Take the case of someone like Jacob. If he's doing both of his jobs well, and his employers are satisfied with his performance — or, less charitably, if they're too dumb to notice his frequent absences — who is he cheating? As he's quick to point out, plenty of other people waste all day at work while they're supposed to be working. He simply optimizes his time better.

Jacob is far from the only person working multiple jobs at the same time. Isaac P. is the anonymous founder of Overemployed (overemployed.com), a website that publishes job reports and updates from multiworking contributors. During the pandemic, he was in the process of changing jobs when he decided to simply stay on at his current one at the same time. He called it a hedge against uncertainty. If the new job didn't work out, he'd still have the old one to fall back on.

He assumed that doing both jobs at once would eventually become too much to handle, forcing him to make a choice. But much to his surprise, he was easily able to perform both roles without having to shirk any responsibilities or cut any corners. When a big layoff hit company #1, his name wasn't on the list. Apparently his bosses had decided he was indispensable. So did it really matter that he was working for them only half the time?

Employment "Hard Mode"

Many video games have a "hard mode" or "expert mode" option, which is typically attempted after players have finished the game on its normal difficulty setting. Taking on multiple full-time jobs is effectively *employment hard mode.*

Multiworking is not quite multitasking—an impossible activity—but rather the continuous management of two or more work environments, projects, and groups of coworkers.

This mode is much easier for some types of professionals than others. The ideal multiworking job is one that requires you to toil away on your own and occasionally poke your head up to report on your progress. If you have a lot of autonomy and are responsible for producing deliverables (code, audits, technical reports) on some sort of schedule, multiworking might be for you.

Even better: if your job is to monitor something that doesn't require much monitoring. IT professionals tend to be overrepresented in this group, at least judging from self-reported info. Noncoding managers don't always know how much—or how little—manual work the people on their teams need to be doing, and clever IT workers can exploit this gap. Also, as we saw with Jacob, working remotely makes it far easier to juggle two sets of tasks and responsibilities.

On the other hand, if the work you do is highly collaborative, this may be harder to pull off. Project managers, leaders of large teams, and anyone else who's expected to work closely with colleagues and be responsive to frequent inquiries could find it difficult to maintain their cover.

For people like Isaac, the founder of Overemployed, multiworking isn't *all* about the extra income; it's also a risk-management strategy.

Contributors to Overemployed—and the nearly 150,000 members of the Overemployed subreddit—refer to their first job as J1, the second as J2, and so on. A typical comment might read: "I was able to be more fearless with J3, because at that point I didn't care about getting fired from J1."* The subreddit is filled with advice and resources for aspiring multiworkers. One thread discusses how

---

* One tip from the community: When applying for new jobs, look out for language like "needs to wear multiple hats," "able to thrive in a fast-paced environment," or even "hands-on." Terms like these are clues that the role requires a high level of involvement—the opposite of what you need for your J2 and beyond.

to make your LinkedIn profile invisible to anyone who works at a particular company, which is helpful when you're already employed but looking for an additional job. Another thread offers reviews of "mouse jigglers:" tiny devices that fit on USB drives and keep your computer screen active, even when you're doing something else.

For these contributors, working *more than two jobs* means they can afford to take the kinds of risks they wouldn't dare take otherwise. In the most extreme example I came across, an IT specialist claimed to hold *five* full-time jobs, all for Fortune 500 companies.

How is such a thing even possible? He simply never stopped interviewing for jobs, and he accepted each offer he received. "If I can keep it up for a year," he wrote, "I'll earn $1.2 million."

This kind of financial cushion doesn't just serve as a safety net; it also provides leverage in negotiations with employers. Each time this IT specialist accepted a new position, he grew more and more emboldened to ask for higher wages. And why not? Clearly, his specialized skills were in high demand, and with paychecks already coming in from multiple companies, he could afford to walk away if he didn't get what he wanted.

Finally, he performed a bold flex with his original employer, telling a manager that meetings were unproductive for him and requesting to be left alone to "focus on his work." He fully expected this audacious demand to be denied—but the manager agreed to it. Clearly, this specialist had mastered a new level of employment hard mode.

Multiple-Job Cheat Sheet: How to Be in Two Places at the Same Time

Who says you can't be in two places at once? For best results, follow these tips.

- Avoid meetings whenever possible. Stave off unwanted meeting invites or spontaneous phone calls by making it clear to your coworkers that you can respond faster and more effectively to other, more asynchronous forms of communication.
- For the meetings you can't weasel out of, avoid video when you can. When you're joining a remote meeting in audio-only mode, you can do other things simultaneously and don't need to keep your eyes on one screen.
- Try to schedule blocks of time dedicated to just one job. During these sessions, make sure that you're available to colleagues and that you're regularly being "seen," whether by speaking up in remote meetings or participating in conversations in digital workspaces like Microsoft Teams or Slack.
- If possible, create a different workspace for each job. Some multiworkers do one job from their home office and another from a desk set up in the living room. This physical separation, even if it's a small one, can help you reset mentally as you transition from one "workday" to another.

- Always use a separate computer for each job. This is crucial. Not only will it help you stay organized, it will also reduce your risk of getting busted. If your company has issued you a laptop or other device to work from, be especially careful: many of them include monitoring software of some kind.

- Don't let yourself get double-booked. Remember that when a colleague from Company A goes into your calendar to schedule a call or meeting with you, they won't be able to see the times you've already committed to a call or meeting for Company B (and vice versa). To avoid an emergency situation where you're expected to be in two places at once, simply block off those times on your calendar and mark them as "busy."

- If you do find yourself in such a situation, attend both meetings using two different devices and toggle back and forth between them (just don't forget to put yourself on mute!). Try to split your attention evenly in case you're asked to speak. If you *are* caught off guard at some point, immediately drop the call and blame the internet connection when you get back on.

- Since you'll be around only half of the time the other employees are (or maybe even less), make sure you're active and available whenever you are. Instead of sending lots of emails in bursts, use the delayed-send feature and schedule them to be sent at random intervals throughout the day. If your jobs use an internal messaging system, keep yourself signed in but set your status to busy, so that if someone messages you and you don't respond, they'll assume you're either in a meeting or buried in your work (and you might be, of course . . . just for another job).

- Discover which tasks are truly urgent at each job and which can wait. Note that some things can wait *perpetually*. Finding tasks that you no longer need to do (ever!) is a huge win, whether you're interested in multiple jobs or just freeing up time in general.
- Keep your social media profiles vague. LinkedIn is especially important: once you've acquired all the jobs you can handle, clean up your profile to remove references to *any* current employer. Unless you're entertaining even more job offers (!), you may also want to make your profile private.
- Finally, decide which job is most important to you. If something came up and you had to choose one tomorrow, which would it be? In the event that one employer learns about the other and forces you to make a decision—you'll already have your answer.

I checked back with Jacob a couple of months after our first interview. He still hadn't been found out, and as far as he could tell, his bosses at both companies were happy with him and his work. There had been a few stressful days where important calls were scheduled at the same time and he'd had to choose which employer to blow off. Afterward, he'd apologized and made an extra effort to be seen online for a while. *No harm done.*

There was one new challenge, though. Project managers at both jobs had begun gently nudging remote workers to use video instead of just audio for meetings—apparently the bosses had determined that participants were more present when their cameras were on. Naturally, this posed a problem for someone who spent most of the meeting time covertly doing something else.

He'd made it a full year as a dual employee, and Jacob was now thinking of retiring from one of his jobs. He wanted to get back to dating, and he missed playing basketball with his friends at the gym. Both of those activities went on pause during the early pandemic days, but now that life was returning to normal, he was ready to reclaim some of his free time.

It was hard to quit his two-job habit, though. Getting multiple large deposits in his bank account every other week was a powerful incentive to keep going. He'd paid off some debt, bought a new truck, and no longer needed to look at prices when he went to restaurants or the grocery store.

Besides, he was enjoying himself. "The cool thing is that I'm not really doing this out of necessity," he said. "I'm doing it out of a desire to maximize my earnings, and also because I like the difficulty of it."

For Jacob, the challenge of multiworking was a feature, not a bug. He talked about how it would be a great story to tell his grandkids one day—by which point he'd presumably have the money to retire in style.

Chapter Five

Playing Video Games for $800/Day

CONCEPT: "Play-to-earn" is a remarkable new mash-up of gaming and finance. It combines financial exchanges with playable online games, complete with quests, collectible characters, and sky-high interest rates on deposits.

When I was in my late teens and early twenties, I was very committed to playing video games. I'd spend hours every evening (and, let's be real, sometimes the middle of the day) honing my skills at games like *Halo* and *Bomberman*.

Unfortunately, no one ever came along to offer me a paycheck for my gaming acumen. It was just a hobby. I eventually got more interested in entrepreneurial projects and stopped gaming for a long time.

Years later, after I had a career as a writer, I would use this example in talks I gave about generating business ideas. "You can't just 'follow your passion' to the bank," I'd say. "Otherwise I would be playing video games for a living!"

That line went over well in 2010. But in the years to come, playing games for a living turned into a real thing.

First came esports, which is now a $2-billion industry fueled by star players, corporate sponsorships, and worldwide broadcasts that attract hundreds of thousands of viewers. Personally, I'm glad the esports trend arrived much later in my gaming life-span. If it had happened in the earlier days, I'm pretty sure I would have lost years of my life trying to make my way into the big league.

Back then, a twenty-something adult who aspired to strike it rich as a professional gamer had about the same odds of success as a basketball player with a dream of playing for the NBA: that is, very low.

Then something came along and changed all that: play-to-earn games, also called GameFi, where players can earn real money for competing in blockchain video games.

In this world, you don't have to be an elite player, land a sponsorship deal, or practice for ten hours a day to monetize your gaming skills. You can just invest a bit of money, log in a couple of times a day to complete a few virtual tasks, and get paid—sometimes a lot.

What Is Play-to-Earn?

If you're familiar with play-to-earn (P2E) games, you may have heard them referred to as *pay*-to-earn, because there's not usually a way to play for free. This is an area where the maxim "It takes money to make money" most certainly applies.

In order to play, gamers typically purchase some form of in-game currency to get started, sometimes along with gaming characters or avatars. They then compete to win in-game assets like tokens, badges, special powers, virtual land, and more. These in-game winnings can be cashed out in the form of currencies like Bitcoin, or even transferred to a traditional bank account after some additional conversion.

The "pay-to-earn" model may not sound like such a great proposition at first. After all, isn't it counterproductive to pay for something that supposedly makes money for you? But keep in mind that millions of people happily pay to play other kinds of video games every day for no profit at all, often spending thousands of dollars on in-game items that have no external value or utility.

Take *Fortnite*, for example, a typical multiplayer game, which has been ranked as the most popular in the world. *Fortnite* often takes in as much as half a billion dollars *a month* from gamers, yet Epic Games, the maker of *Fortnite*, doesn't share any of that money with players. If you've ever played games like *Fortnite*, *Diablo*, *World of Warcraft*, *Civilization*, or *Final Fantasy* (the list could go on . . .), just imagine if you could blend that experience with the added incentive of a financial return.

If you think about the world of "pay-to-earn" as a place where gaming meets financial markets (hence the term *GameFi*, although *play-to-earn* and *play-and-earn* are now more commonly used), the model starts to make a lot more sense.

With those more traditional titles, you're investing money in return for the hours of enjoyment you'll get from playing the game. In the play-to-earn world, you can still enjoy the experience, but you're also investing money that you can put to work in the service of making *more* money, just as you would by investing in the stock market, or in some asset like gold or real estate.

Moreover, with games like *Fortnite*, which exist in a siloed ecosystem controlled by the game's developers, the tokens and badges and other digital assets you win have no value outside the walled garden of the game. But with play-to-earn games, which operate without any centralized authority, players control these digital assets, which they can transfer or trade outside the game as they please. In this way, GameFi also represents a new kind of ownership economy, in which players can build equity on their investment via in-game assets.

Sure, most traditional investments don't involve Pokémon-like creatures that you send into battle to get paid, but think of it this way: According to general estimates, something like 56 percent of Americans own stocks, whereas only about 10 to 15 percent have investments in digital currencies like Bitcoin. Yet a full *71 percent* play video games of some kind. What this suggests is that GameFi has the potential to reach a much larger group of people beyond the ones who are already into investing.

Get paid to play video games. As you can probably tell, I was hooked.

The Billion-Dollar Blockchain Game Run by Cartoon Characters

The GameFi trend can trace its rise to a single game, *Axie Infinity*.* At its peak, Axie had something like two million people playing at once. Many of them were in countries like the Philippines and Venezuela, where they could earn more from playing the game than they could from available job opportunities.

I didn't play *Axie* myself, but I thought it was pretty cool that so many people (especially in poorer countries) were making real money from it.

To get started, a player would buy several "Axies," which were cute, Pokémon-like creatures ready to be deployed into battle against other players in sets of three. If your team won the battle, you would receive a token, AXS, which had real monetary value and could be withdrawn and exchanged for dollars or any other currency.

As the game took off, more and more people invested in Axies and the underlying token. The price of AXS exploded, turning

---

* Technically, both *Axie* and many other games were inspired by an earlier project called *Cryptokitties*. As much as I love cats, we'll have to leave that story for another time.

into one of the best investments you could have made in 2020. A $100 investment in the early days of Axie was worth $17,000 one year later. By comparison, a $100 investment in Amazon, which was up 70 percent that same year, would have been worth $170. Clearly, you would have been much better off putting your money in a video game.

Ready Player One

Axie was a huge success, but it had a glaring problem: the gameplay sucked. To put it another way, there *was* no real gameplay. There was no strategy to master, no puzzle to solve. Once you sent your Axies into battle, there wasn't much to do except watch the cartoon characters duke it out and wait for the result. And because the game was built with a mandatory cooldown period, you then had to wait some more before you could send your Axies back out onto the battlefield.

It was, however, an innovative first-mover concept that pointed the way to something better.

Sensing an opportunity, other new and existing video game makers quickly moved in to create their own play-to-earn platforms. The stakes were high: The right game could attract tens of millions of dollars in investment in a matter of days. Even a bad one (and there were many of those) could be profitable for the creators. In less than six months, a bountiful assortment of strategy games, fantasy games, card-collecting games, and all sorts of other genres had popped up.

It was around this time that I discovered *DeFi Kingdoms*, a play-to-earn game in the style of an old-school role-playing game. Unlike what I'd seen of *Axie* (at least in the beginning; the company has since added new features), *DeFi Kingdoms* felt like a real game. The characters I acquired had dozens of unique attributes, all of which came with lots of stats to monitor and modify. When I leveled up, I had a choice as to which abilities to maximize.

I'd started gaming again during the pandemic, but soon found my PlayStation gathering dust while I remained glued to my laptop playing *DeFi Kingdoms* for hours.

It produced a familiar sense of dopamine rewards tied to in-game actions. I fished and foraged for new items, I explored new lands, I leveled up my characters, called *heroes*, which in turn made them more powerful for battles.

There was just one difference: after making an initial investment and learning the gameplay, I was making hundreds of dollars a day for my efforts.

So yeah, that was cool.

Soon *DeFi Kingdoms* was an ecosystem of more than 50,000 heroes, all held in wallets belonging to players. You could send your heroes out on quests, from which they'd bring back items and level up their stats, thus becoming more valuable. Or you could try your hand at earning more Jewel (the main in-game currency) by reselling items or heroes to other players in the game's online marketplace.

The money earned by players, in other words, came from two sources: first, the in-game winnings, and second, the buying pressure from other players that pushed up the value of the assets as they transacted. The biggest return of all could be found in the *DeFi Kingdoms* gardens, where you could "stake" your Jewel along with another in-game currency and earn interest on it every day.

How much interest? When I entered the game, the APR was more than 600 percent. You earned this passive income by depositing two coins in equal amounts, both the native Jewel and another token like Bitcoin or Ethereum. The two tokens made a "liquidity pool," which offered daily rewards in the form of Jewel. Or, if you preferred, you could skip the token-pairing process and just keep your Jewel in the in-game bank, where it would earn interest at the rate of "only" around 250 percent.

If this model sounds familiar, that's because it's more or less how normal banks operate. You loan them money, usually in the form of a deposit, and earn interest in return. The only difference was that banks in the real world were offering something like *one* percent interest.

Naturally, I was intrigued. There was just one catch: high interest rates tend to come with high amounts of risk—as I learned the hard way a bit later.

"Because crypto"

Here's a funny thing: four months after launching, *DeFi King-doms* had more than $1 billion (yep) in total deposits, and the game's creators were completely anonymous. *No one knew who was running the show.*

Imagine a billion-dollar start-up run by anonymous executives. The idea is ludicrous, right? Yet that's how it works with many projects that live on a decentralized (i.e., blockchain) platform, including play-to-earn games.

As a player (effectively a shareholder), you have no idea who the game developers (the people in charge) are or where they're based. Most teams say they have security controls in place, but you have to take their word for it. There's no customer service line to call, no tech support to contact, no way to report bugs or glitches. Just an anonymous avatar who, in the case of *DeFi Kingdoms,* went by the name Frisky Fox. Other members of the creative team—the developers, designers, and so on—adopted monikers like Beetle Dude, Pie Face, Professor Tango, and Raspberry Swirl.

Why would these people not want to identify themselves and take credit for the game they created? "Because crypto" is the nonanswer most people gave me when I posed this question. It's true that many people in the crypto world prefer to be anonymous. Anonymity is central to the ethos, and these currencies were designed to preserve it from the very beginning. But since so much money (not to mention significant bragging rights) was at stake, it still seemed unusual to me.

AUTHOR'S PLAY-TO-EARN

MORNING WORK SCHEDULE

In the early days of my *DeFi Kingdoms* obsession, back when I had just a few heroes to play with, I would check in with the game for a few minutes every morning, but there wasn't much for me to do.

As my collection grew and as I expanded my strategy, however, I found myself spending more and more time attending to my virtual kingdom. It was basically like owning a fast-moving business!

With other ventures I've run, my morning to-do list would include items like checking sales reports, responding to any urgent communication, and setting up a product mailing.

In my new career as a semiprofessional gamer, a typical morning began with a very different kind of work. My list of tasks looked something like this:

- Collect heroes from the overnight shift.
- Send out fishers and foragers to bring back new items.
- Send mining teams out to search for gold.

- Level up any heroes who have achieved sufficient XP (experience points).
- Claim rewards (interest) from the gardens and in-game bank.
- Compound earnings and redeposit to gardens.
- List heroes for sale in the tavern (the in-game marketplace).
- Check on any interesting new hero listings.
- Skim the game's Discord and subreddit to learn of any new features or updates.

In short, it's not easy taking care of a virtual kingdom. But I'm not complaining, because most of the time this was a profitable activity. It was also a lot of fun.

Rich Crab, Poor Crab

Playing around with *DeFi Kingdoms* soon led me to another play-to-earn game. This one was built around an undersea world featuring factions of hermit crabs, all battling for control. It was called *Crabada*, and I got interested in it because the ROI was simple: buy some crabs, enter them in battles or put them to work on various quests and tasks, and earn in-game tokens that could be converted to dollars.

Yes, this meant I was now investing in virtual crabs at prices that started around $500 and went up into the thousands. But if all variables remained constant, I'd earn back my investment within two months. What could go wrong?

Spoiler: a lot could go wrong when the crab market crashed. But we'll come back to that later.

The week I discovered *Crabada*, I was traveling in Vietnam. I started off with a couple of crab teams that worked as miners. Practically speaking, this meant I had to log on a few times a day to complete some chores: sending crabs to the mines, collecting them upon return, and fending off other players trying to loot the mines and steal much of my profit.

Like any good GameFi project, *Crabada* offered multiple ways to earn. You could send your crabs to the mines, as I was doing. You could also rent out your crabs in a virtual tavern, where other players would hire them as reinforcements for their missions—think of them as the mercenaries of the crustacean kingdom.

Or you could become a breeder. This required purchasing "virgin" crabs that had never been bred, allowing them to mate, then waiting five days for a virtual crab egg to hatch. Once the time had passed, *voilà!* You'd have a new crab that was ready to go to work.

Finally, you could join the ranks of the looters, which was more profitable, but also more time-consuming. Looters could raid miners every other hour, whereas miners could go to work only every four hours. You didn't *have* to work twelve shifts a day as a looter, but the more you logged on, the more money you made. The game's economics rewarded players who put in the time.

After I'd acquired a few mining teams, I decided to cast my nets in deeper waters. I went to the online marketplace and purchased a set of virgin crabs. Over the next few weeks I dutifully visited my breeding stable, hatched my crabs, put them in the marketplace to sell, and started the cycle again with a new batch.

My day was suddenly getting very busy. I was still playing the other game, so I now had to manage bands of medieval heroes *and* teams of virtual crabs, while also keeping up with new forum threads to increase my knowledge of strategy. This was on top of other responsibilities, like writing this book and recording my podcast, so it was sometimes a struggle to fit it all in.

New Goal: Play with the House's Money

Was all of this profitable? It depends. By this point I had expanded my crabbing operation to seven teams, and each team earned around $12 per mining shift. Teams were eligible to begin a shift every four hours, so at maximum efficiency that would mean I'd be earning several hundred dollars a day.* But

---

* And as long as I didn't sleep more than four hours at a time. Whenever I missed a rotation, my daily income declined. :(

because the game provided so many additional ways to supplement my mining income, on some days I logged on in the morning and withdrew $800 or more in profits from the previous day's earnings. That felt good.

But the market was also highly volatile. The in-game economy is tied to cryptocurrencies, which meant that when those currencies lost value, so did my assets. And when Bitcoin slumped, the smaller "altcoins" used in the game fell even more. Some days I saw the value of my virtual holdings drop by an uncomfortable amount. That's why I came to realize a very important strategy for play-to-earn: instead of holding on to your investments for the long haul, as is typically a wise strategy for traditional assets like stocks or real estate, in the world of GameFi, you should try to get back your original investment (i.e., "get to ROI") as quickly as possible.

The real goal was to go "revenue-positive"—a point at which I'd withdrawn enough in profit to recoup my original investment. After that, I'd be playing with the house's money. If my miners continued to earn, that was great: I could take that income and use it to bankroll other projects without harming my initial investment. And if Bitcoin crashed and sent everything else down with it, at least my initial outlay would be safe.

It turned out that withdrawing my earnings once I hit this point required great self-discipline. Just like in the stock market, it was hard to refrain from putting more money into an investment that was working well. If you made $10,000 one month, why not try for $20,000 the next? All you had to do was double down by adding more capital.

This line of thinking seems logical enough, but as any savvy investor will tell you, the worst time to buy into a market is at the top. The smarter play is to set limits and not worry about "all the money you're not making" — that's a faulty way of thinking. Plus, because every digital currency is prone to wide swings in value, doubling down increases your exposure to risk even further.

Lesson learned: When the price spikes, resist the temptation to go all-in. Take profits instead.

A CRAB IN THE HAND . . .

Withdrawing profits regularly is a key move that separates pros from amateurs. Here are a few tips.

1. *Set price limits.* If your favorite game token costs $4 and its value rises to $12, should you sell, or stick with it in the hope that it keeps rising? It's easy to get caught up in the heat of the moment and think *Let it ride!*

To avoid making this kind of emotional decision, decide in advance at what point you'll claw back your profits, and make yourself stick to it.

2. *Make incremental withdrawals.* When you earn interest on an investment in the regular financial markets, it makes sense to reinvest that income to compound the earnings. But remember, these games trade in currencies far more volatile than most savings accounts. So in this case, it's often better to withdraw a portion of your profits at least once a week until you've "earned out" your investment. Once you do, you're in a great position to take more risk if you so choose.

3. *Keep records.* The tax laws for crypto are confusing, especially once you start using your own wallet instead of going through a centralized exchange like Coinbase or Binance. But you *do* have to pay taxes on these earnings, so keep some sort of ledger of major purchases and withdrawals. Once you start making real money, ask a tax advisor about the best way to take distributions.

4. *Consider it your job (or at least one of your jobs).* If you really did play games for a living, you'd have some sort of regular salary, which means you'd get a paycheck week after week, regardless of how much work you produced or how much time you put in. But with the play-to-earn model, you're less like a salaried employee and more like a sales professional paid entirely in commission. Even if the amount you make on each sale may vary, the more time you spend pounding the pavement, the more income you will generate.

In short, pay yourself! If I could go back in time to the start of my gaming-for-money days, I would make a plan to do that from the beginning.

Play-to-Earn: The Next Frontier

Play-to-earn exploded during the pandemic, providing a fun and lucrative diversion for people stuck at home. Though the industry shrank considerably with the rest of the crypto crash, new games continued to launch.

In some cases, these games can still be viable investments, albeit highly volatile ones. To stem the criticism, some game makers began to use the term *play*-and-*earn*, embracing a "gameplay first" ethos in which the earning component was secondary. When I tried out one such game called *Mars Colony* (which is exactly what it sounds like), I was greeted with a welcome screen that included the disclaimer, "This is not a financial product" in bold text.

Funny enough, this nonfinancial product still required real money to play. Those biofuel stations and planetary rovers don't come cheap!

Play-to-Earn Tips

- **Get in early-ish.** Yes, the people who truly get in on the ground floor of a new game can do fabulously well—at least if the game becomes a hit. But your rewards will still be high, and your risk will be much lower, if you get in after some momentum is established but before the game really takes off. That's why early-*ish* is good *(we'll look at the "early-ish" concept in another chapter as well).*

Too early	Early-ish	Too late
"I've never heard of anything like this!"	"I should get in on this before it takes off!"	"Everyone is talking about this!"

- **Dive deep.** If you want to take play-to-earn seriously, be prepared to do a lot of reading on forums like Reddit, Discord, and Medium. There's real skill involved. The more you understand about the **mechanics**—that is, the specific gaming tasks, options, and choices available to players—the more likely you are to spot the best and most profitable strategies.

If you think these games sound simple, think again. Like chess or poker, the best modern games can be easy to pick up and play but require dozens of hours to master. Play-to-earn games are no different. It took me about a month of reading and exploring for at least an hour or two a day before I had a solid grasp of *DeFi Kingdoms,* for example.

- **Pay attention to momentum.** Not all play-to-earn games will stand the test of time, and with more and more coming onto the market, it's inevitable that a growing number of them will flop. To protect against losses, you should always be on the lookout for signs that a game might be losing its momentum.

If a game goes for months and months without any new updates, that may mean that its creators are getting ready to throw in the towel and move on. Similarly, a plateauing user base is a sure sign of concern. Monitor the number of active users, and notice the growth trends. Slow and steady gains tend to be better than a huge influx of new players all at once, although spikes in new users can also inspire price spikes as more people rush to buy items and characters.

Most play-to-earn games have strong network effects, which means that their value to you increases along with the number of people who use it. So if you sense that the enthusiasm from other players is lagging, for example, don't ignore the feeling. Trust your intuition when it tells you it might be time to quit.

- **Pick a lane.** Most play-to-earn games offer more than one way to get paid. Should you specialize, or do some of everything?

The best answer: In the beginning, go wide and learn as much as you can about the whole game. Eventually, though, go deep and focus your efforts on a couple of preferred strategies.

■ **Don't forget basic internet security.** Never share your wallet password or recovery phrase, *especially* with someone who claims to be with a help desk. This is almost always a scam. Don't click on random links, especially any of them that request approval to connect with your online wallet.

Oh, and one more thing to look out for with play-to-earn gaming: it can take over your life. You might find yourself getting up in the middle of the night to send your heroes out on quests.

A GAMEFI GLOSSARY

If you want to play video games for real money, there's a lot to learn, starting with the lingo. (Note: some of these terms apply to other projects in crypto, not just gaming.)

Tokenomics — All the elements that determine a currency's value, including how existing tokens are distributed, as well as when any new tokens will be created. You can usually find a published white paper with the details for any token. If the material seems dense, read the analysis of the material written by experts. They'll usually break down the most important parts.

Days to ROI—How long it takes to become profitable with a particular strategy, given the current economics of the game.

Mint—A sale of NFTs, tokens, or some other limited asset that has utility in the game or project. Before an asset is minted, the event is usually announced and hyped well in advance. Players who get in early have the chance to benefit from price appreciation (though of course the price can also drop if the mint doesn't go well).

Whitelist—Some mints are open only to participants who meet certain criteria, such as already owning an NFT or having a minimum amount of money in the game. The developers keep track of these "whitelisted" participants, giving them early access or some other advantage in the purchase process.

Airdrop—A reward provided to participants who meet certain conditions. These can be announced in advance or delivered as a surprise. When you receive an airdrop, you typically need to "claim" it to add it to your wallet.

Scholarship plan—Just as it sounds, some games have a program that allows players with limited funds to participate. It's not exactly free money; the scholarship players are essentially renting characters from players who've invested larger amounts. When it's designed appropriately, however, it can be a win-win for both groups.

What Could Go Wrong?

Not everyone thinks play-to-earn is amazing. Some think it's bad for gaming, bad for finance, and too addictive.

Personally, I wouldn't go that far. But the barriers to entry *are* real: To participate in most play-to-earn games, an investment of several hundred dollars is the bare minimum. To actively compete costs much more. And while plenty of people make back that investment, no winning streak lasts forever—at least not without encountering some bumps in the road.

Beginning with the original play-to-earn platform, *Axie Infinity*, almost every game has run into the same problem: the model struggles when the number of new players fails to keep up with the inflationary growth of in-game assets. And while for a time it seemed the price of Axies would always go up, eventually the trend reversed. Investing in Axies felt more like a meme stock: a high-risk idea with an uncertain reward.

Players love that the breeding function in most of these games allows them to build up a large stable of characters for earning or reselling. The problem is that as more and more game characters are introduced, supply eventually outpaces demand, and the price goes off a cliff. It's difficult to avoid this "runaway economy" because players are incentivized to breed more, and because the game's economy relies on fees from breeding and sales. All you can do to protect yourself is to watch for the signs that free fall is imminent and get out—fast—before too much damage is done.

At its peak, Axie's AXS token traded at $164. A year later, it hovered around $38. Three months after that, it cratered to $12.

Earlier I mentioned that *DeFi Kingdoms* had 50,000 in-game characters when I started playing. In a matter of months, the ranks had swelled to more than 100,000. There simply weren't enough new players to accommodate the surge in supply, however, so prices dropped. It was still possible to make money from the game, but not nearly as much.

Two other phenomena accelerated the decline of both games, and many more like them: the death spiral and the sleeping dragon. A death spiral is pretty much what it sounds like. When the price of an asset crashes, it doesn't usually recover. Because no one wants to invest in an asset on a downward trajectory, it's simply more likely to keep going down than it is to reverse direction.

If inflationary breeding leads to a death spiral, the death spiral leads to what's known as the sleeping dragon. When the price drops rapidly, lots of players panic and sell, but others hold on. After a certain point, they think, *Well, if I sell now I'll have a huge loss, so I'll just wait until the price recovers.*

This is logical enough, but the problem is that if a large number of players are holding on to these assets—whether in the form of characters, tokens, or both—the price will eventually begin to rally a bit. That's when the sleeping dragon awakens, players cash out, and another sell-off occurs.

This pattern is sometimes described as *ponzinomics,* referring to the fact that new players end up buying these assets, thereby providing exit liquidity for the players who cash out at a profit while they still can.

It's very, very difficult to overcome this pattern once it sets in.

The forums of *Axie* players are cluttered with posts of people announcing that they are leaving the game, having failed to find their fortune. "It's not fun to click over and over for pennies" is a common complaint. Another is that these games are unfair or even rigged.

As a longtime gamer, I understood these arguments. At the same time, I thought they missed the point. The truth is that, just like many old-school video games, blockchain games like *DeFi Kingdoms* offered complexity that rewarded astute players. If you studied and responded quickly to changes in game mechanics, you'd advance. And to me, someone who was interested in both gaming and entrepreneurship, the fact that you could be rewarded financially for doing so was the whole point.

Critics of the model tend to miss another important fact. Play-to-earn is more volatile than the stock market, but the fact that price movement in either direction carries benefit for some group of shareholders is the same. Unlike stocks or other assets (even cryptocurrency), the in-game assets continue to have some utility and earning potential even if the price craters.

I eventually stopped earning hundreds of dollars a day in *DeFi Kingdoms,* but even once the value of the token fell off a cliff, my heroes could still earn $30 to $50 a day for their daily mining. They weren't nearly as profitable as before, but they still earned *something*. I could sell them and move on, or I could just wait and see if the tide turned.

Meanwhile, when the value of in-game assets falls, so does the barrier to enter the game. This isn't great for existing players who bought in at the top, but it's ideal for new players. Instead of spending thousands of dollars on a trio of virtual crabs, they could snatch them up for $100 or less.

As for me, I'm still actively playing several play-to-earn games on a daily basis. Sadly, I lost money in *Crabada*, having bought in at peak crab. In *DeFi Kingdoms*, the token price crashed, but I still turned a profit from the stable of sixty heroes that I'd acquired.

Overall, I did surprisingly well, especially once I reallocated some of my time from fishing and mining in my medieval kingdom to collecting eggs on virtual farmland in a new game called *Chikn* (tagline: "everyone knows that Chikn lay $EGG"). That endeavor produced a 300 percent return on investment, and my virtual chickens and roosters continue to thrive on their virtual farm.

I always dreamed of getting paid to play video games. I thought I'd missed my chance, but it turns out I wasn't born too early after all.

Chapter Six

The Revolution Will Be Livestreamed

CONCEPT: Livestreaming and making on-demand videos for fans can be a big business, one that offers scale and reach to talented creators.

Jakey Boehm works the night shift, but he tries to sleep through it.

The Australian is a self-described sleepfluencer, who gets paid to livestream his attempts at sleeping through the night. *Attempts* is a key word, because his whole business model revolves around viewers contributing virtual gift items — purchased, of course, with real money — that trigger all sorts of disruptions.

Want to pipe a loud air horn, or perhaps a siren, into his bedroom? That's easy enough; just send over a gift item and you'll hear your reward on the stream within seconds.

Send more virtual gifts and you can watch Jakey attempt to sleep through flashing disco lights, a fake FBI raid, a medley of techno tracks played at high volume, a fifteen-second spray of bubbles, and even a bouncing blow-up piñata, which Boehm attacks in dramatic fashion upon his awakening.

Yes, people pay for these things. And yes, Boehm is able to redeem the virtual gifts for real dollars that get deposited in his bank account. TikTok sets up the system in a gamified way that subtly disguises the transactional nature of the exchange. Instead of just chipping in $25 to keep the techno track going, you have to buy a virtual item (for $25) called "I'm Very Rich." This token then goes to Boehm, who can trade it for diamonds (another virtual item) and then cash out from there. This is not just something he does every once in a while when he's short on cash. He does it every night, seven days a week. *It's his job.*

At first his income was sporadic, but as his following grew, Boehm began making $1,000 a week, then $5,000. At the time I talked with him, he'd amassed nearly half a million followers and had recently earned $49,000 in a single month.

For everyone who thinks being interrupted all night sounds like a terrible way to make a living, just consider: if Boehm were to keep earning at that rate, he'd be making close to $600,000 a year. At that salary, most of us might be willing to plan for a few naps to make up the sleep deficit.*

Boehm isn't the only sleepfluencer on TikTok, though he's

---

* Or you could make it all an act. Plan for the night shift to be your true working hours, even if you spend them entirely in bed, swatting away piñatas and listening to techno music that your followers have paid for. Then, during the day, you sleep in your real bedroom, free of disco lights and bubble streamers. It's a living.

certainly the only one I found who's taken it to such a bizarre level. Other sleepfluencers are more interested in, well, *sleeping,* and stream themselves doing so through the night without distractions. Viewers can still contribute gift items, but the point isn't to jolt the sleeper out of peaceful slumber, but rather to set a model for healthy sleep.

Media profiles of Boehm inevitably include a quote from a health professional who warns about the "dangers" of Boehm's nighttime habits. *Tsk tsk.* Who cares? He's twenty-eight years old. He knows this gig isn't going to last forever.

When it ends, he'll have an incredible story to tell of how he earned tens of thousands of dollars a week by letting strangers on the internet disturb his sleep.

Miss Excel, the Spreadsheet TikTok Star

When the pandemic lockdowns began in the spring of 2020, people all across the world suddenly found themselves with extra time on their hands. To keep themselves occupied—and perhaps distracted from the grim realities playing out around them— many people took up new hobbies. Some baked sourdough. Others knit scarves, did puzzles, or adopted puppies.

But many more logged in to TikTok and started filming. For some creators, posting silly videos was just a fun pastime. For others, it was a low-stakes way to share their expertise, experience, or knowledge with those who might benefit from it. And for some clever creators, it turned out to be an unexpected path to wealth and stardom.

One such creator is Kat Norton, but most people call her Miss Excel. She is perhaps the first true "Microsoft Office Influencer," as odd as that sounds. Nearly every day she posts a new video featuring a tip on using Excel or other spreadsheet apps.

These videos get 50,000 views on average, but the ones that go viral receive eight times as many. Who knew spreadsheets could be so interesting?

A few recent video topics:

- "Are gridlines cramping your style?"
- "Stop using pivot tables!"
- "This data is messy AF"
- "Excel magic with the ALT keys"
- "Secret cell trick will change ya life"

In many of her short videos, Norton doesn't even speak. Instead, she dances in the lower two-thirds of the frame while spreadsheet tips float in and out above her. That's it! One video featured Norton doing the "Spreadsheet Shuffle," a dance she created. In another, she's dancing underneath a tutorial about how to separate text into columns.

Behind Miss Excel's dance-offs, there's a sophisticated business model. In some videos, she invites viewers to join for a free training, in keeping with the tried-and-true format of webinar salesmanship: give people helpful information, answer their questions, then pitch them on a paid version. It's hard to see where the line is between entertainment, education, and sales—which is exactly the point.

Long ago I wrote about a guy in India who went by the name Mr. Spreadsheet. When I interviewed him, he'd built a successful lifestyle business and was earning a bit more than $100,000 a year—a good living, especially in India—by blogging his Excel tips and selling templates that would help users save time at work (no dancing was involved).

A decade later, however, Miss Excel was attracting an exponentially larger audience and smashing all previous income records in my made-up category of "spreadsheet influencers." As I was working on this book, Miss Excel shared a post announcing her first $100,000 *day*.

No kidding. In a single day, she'd sold six figures in online courses, which typically have a profit margin exceeding 90 percent. Thanks to TikTok, her project operated on a scale of engagement that simply wasn't possible until recently.

Compared to YouTube, which also hosts plenty of livestreamers and creators, TikTok is an amateur's paradise. Historically, YouTube has rewarded creators who take the time to make detailed, more-produced videos.

TikTok is different. For one thing, short videos like the ones Miss Excel creates don't require much production time; in fact, many of the most successful videos on TikTok are deliberately *under*produced. Whereas YouTube rewards quality and quantity, TikTok rewards zaniness, spontaneity, and authenticity.

In gaining the attention of so many followers, Kat Norton had achieved something remarkable: turning Excel spreadsheets into a meme. There really is an audience for anything.

The Lockpicking Lawyer

If TikTok is a land of opportunity for amateur creators, YouTube is where you go if you have a unique skill you want to monetize. In Damascus, Maryland, a YouTuber known only as the Lockpicking Lawyer runs one of the most interesting and unusual channels I've ever seen. This channel consists exclusively of short videos where he picks every type of lock imaginable and breaks down the strengths and weaknesses of various security devices.

That's right—all he does is pick locks, over and over. He also speaks in a monotonous cadence that is basically the opposite of a dynamic presenter.* In the videos, you never see his face; his hands and various lock-picking tools take up the full frame.

It bucks the conventional wisdom about content creation (be upbeat and charismatic and look straight into the camera), and

---

* Let's just say the stand-alone audio from his videos wouldn't be ineffective as a sleep meditation.

yet—it works. More than four million people subscribe to the Lockpicking Lawyer's channel. Viewers sometimes send in challenges in the form of purportedly unpickable locks, international locks, keypad "smart locks," and bottles of expensive scotch that require solving a puzzle lock to open. The Lockpicking Lawyer picks them all, and quickly.

He now works as a consultant to the security industry and sells his own lock-picking tools to eager viewers hoping to replicate his experiments.

I'm not enthralled with the world of locksmithing, but while writing this short section I hopped over to his channel and ended up spending half an hour watching him reveal the shortfalls of many leading models of bike locks. Once you're *locked in*, it's hard to look away.

The College Dropout Who Gives Away Millions

Ask anyone who watches YouTube, especially any man under the age of thirty, and they'll know Jimmy Donaldson, who goes by MrBeast. If this guy's story was written into a novel or screenplay, an editor would cut it on the grounds of its being completely implausible. But he's not a fictional character, he's a twenty-five-year-old college dropout living in Greenville, North Carolina.

Donaldson got his start with what sounds like the most boring video stunt imaginable: he counted to 100,000, on camera. It took forty hours and was then condensed into a mere twenty-four-hour video for YouTube. From there, he turned this bizarre theme into a series. He went through the same drive-through a thousand times in a row. He read every word in the dictionary out loud. He attempted to spin a fidget spinner without stopping, for an entire day.

His dedication to absurd tasks that required superhuman stamina was a big part of what helped his fame grow. As his videos continued racking up views, he began raking in lucrative brand sponsorships.

And as his wealth grew alongside the fame, Donaldson saw the opportunity for even wilder — and more expensive — stunts. He approached strangers and handed them $10,000 in cash. He tipped waitresses and Uber drivers thousands of dollars. He sold his mansion for a dollar. Time and again, he seemed to have no hesitation in giving away massive amounts of money. Perhaps it helped that he quickly made it back through advertising and sales of MrBeast-branded merchandise.

These grandiose acts of benevolence increased his fame even further. At the time of writing, Donaldson has more than 100 million followers, enough to place him in the top ten most-followed creators on the platform. More than sixty people are now employed by the Beast empire, and in May 2022 Donaldson was featured on the cover of *Rolling Stone* (naturally, he was pictured lying in a sea of cash).

According to the most recent estimate of his income, he earns at least $3 million a month from ads and partnerships. "Once you know how to make a video go viral, you can practically make unlimited money," he said in an interview with Bloomberg News.

When Donaldson got his 100 millionth subscriber, he bought a private island, where he staged an elaborate challenge that required contestants to start a fire with rocks before competing in a *Squid Game*–style Red Light, Green Light game.* And despite a slew of negative media articles, his audience—and his wealth—just kept on growing. As of July 2022, his videos had been viewed over 25 billion times, spawning a whole new generation of YouTube creators who make money by filming themselves giving away money.

Livestreaming May Be Fleeting, But "Hot Takes" Can Live Forever

If you're planning to become a viral video star, there's one major decision you need to make early on: Are you more of a livestreamer, or more of a video creator?

Some of the answer has to do with which platform you choose.

---

* In an important modification, instead of being killed, the losers of MrBeast's Red Light, Green Light game walked away with a $3,000 consolation prize.

Twitch is all about streaming. YouTube offers both streaming and on-demand videos but is better suited to the latter. The same is true with TikTok and Instagram: they have streaming options, but—at least for now—tend to favor videos that stay up for viewers to watch anytime.

In the world of on-demand videos, there's also a fairly clear distinction between highly produced content and "hot takes," which feature creators speaking direct-to-camera in a more informal manner and setting. But while they may seem completely off-the-cuff and spontaneous, in many cases they have been meticulously scripted and practiced in order to appear that way. Editing and producing video is a skill that's easy to learn but hard to master. Ideally, it should look effortless, even when it actually requires hours of preparation and work for each minute on camera.

Livestreaming, on the other hand, is, as the name suggests, live. There are no second takes and there is no editing—viewers are watching something real in real time.

Sleepfluencer Jakey Boehm is a true livestreamer. Miss Excel's videos, in contrast, are available on demand. Rebecca Rogers, the social studies teacher profiled in chapter two, does hot takes almost exclusively. Again, there's some overlap between these styles, but most creators specialize in one or the other.

For many creators, the videos themselves aren't the real moneymakers. "I had a video get twelve million views and I may have made three or four hundred bucks off of it," Rogers told me.

But successful creators can earn exponentially more from partnerships than they can from the direct payments some receive for their videos — just like pro athletes with promo deals that vastly eclipse their large contracts to play a sport.

That said, getting paid requires more than just getting attention. That's why, in addition to building a following, successful livestreamers and video creators also need to build a *business*.

Miss Excel, for example, packaged her material into courses and sells them at premium prices. Jakey Boehm, on the other hand, pushes his audience to buy more gift items. "Don't let me sleep!" an AI-generated voiceover tells viewers during lulls in his streams.

Over on YouTube, the Lockpicking Lawyer gently promotes sales of his own set of tools and accessories. Instead of simply pointing out the tools he uses for each video, he'll say something like "Here I'm going to use this tool that you can buy at covertinstruments.com." These mentions come frequently enough to remain in the viewer's mind, but not so often that they start to get annoying, or sound like ads.

Once the business model is established, however, creators still need to focus on bringing in more viewers. After all, the more views you get, the more you can sell (or in the case of brand sponsorship, the more you'll get paid to endorse products). Make videos, grow the audience, get paid — that's how it works.

"Smash that subscribe button!"
(Tips for YouTube, TikTok, and beyond)

If you ask kids what they want to be when they grow up, these days they're just as likely to choose influencer as they are astronaut or doctor. In a recent survey of ten-year-olds, influencer was named among the top ten professions, along with DJ and rapper (baseball player and pilot, however, have been crowded out).

But how many of these kids will actually be able to earn a living from their online celebrity? It's true that platforms like TikTok, Twitch, and others have made it easier than ever for pretty much anyone to become at least a little bit "internet famous," but surely there's a limit somewhere — and there are only so many brand sponsorships and advertiser dollars to go around.

YouTube is full of videos about how to get famous on YouTube — mostly by people who've seemingly cracked the algorithm (i.e., their videos get recommended to lots of people) and claim to know the secret. But more often than not, they revert to generic advice: make high-quality videos, connect with your audience, and keep putting out content. These are all good things to do, but plenty of creators check all those boxes and don't hit it big.

Just like most high school basketball players won't make the NBA, most creators won't get paid millions of dollars to pick locks or read the dictionary out loud. Still, whereas most people aren't going to become millionaire sleepfluencers, there's room for all sorts of new ideas that don't yet exist. If you want to improve your odds of getting discovered, these tips should help.

1. **Be first, sort of.** Look at popular creators you like and think, *How can I be similar but also different?* Whatever your answer is, it doesn't necessarily have to appeal to the largest possible audience. As we've seen, the weirder and more niche, the better; you can't simply do the exact same thing someone else did and expect the same results. You need to understand why their strategy worked so well, then find a unique twist of your own.

2. **Recognize that some topics are more profitable than others.** Miss Excel is crushing it because the courses she offers aren't just fun; they teach skills that will help you work much faster and save time every day. That's valuable!

   While I was studying up on creators, I began following one who used a model similar to Miss Excel's, only these videos were about caring for houseplants. That creator also had a large following and sold courses every day, but for only $20 to $40 each instead of $200+ each.

   Don't get me wrong—people want to know how not to kill their houseplants, and they'll pay for that knowledge. They just don't value it as much as something that relates directly to saving time in the workplace.

3. **Focus on projecting personality as much (if not more) than knowledge.** Personality and warmth are important, often underestimated parts of what attracts people to your content and keeps them watching. These qualities might seem frustratingly subjective and hard to measure — "You just need the right vibe," one creator told me — but whatever the *x* factor is, it matters.

   A friend sent me a link to a video by Ryan Trahan, a young creator undertaking a series of social experiments. "There's something about him that's so endearing," my friend said. And there was, so I kept watching. But you don't have to dust off your acting skills or pretend to be something you aren't. With all the mountains of content out there, a unique, authentic personality can be the factor that sets you apart from other creators doing equally cool and creative things.

4. **Plan ahead.** Not sure what topic to make your next video on? Brainstorm lots of ideas in advance, and always keep a list on hand.

   Remember, a lot of the most popular videos you'll find on these platforms may *seem* casual and off-the-cuff, but in fact, they took a good amount of planning and effort to do well. Counterintuitive as it might sound, if you want to come across as spontaneous and unplanned, it pays to plan ahead.

5. **Be consistent, and stick to a schedule.** Creators who are consistent don't attract just more fans. They also attract more *engaged* fans — the type who come back again and again. These are also the fans who pay closer attention, so make sure you publish consistently, whether it's daily, biweekly, or something else. Once people get used to your regular cadence, they'll come to expect it. So if you don't consistently stick to that schedule, you're at risk of losing a big part of your audience.

6. **Include a "call to action."** There's a reason why so many YouTube creators begin their videos by saying "If you like this video, give it a thumbs-up...and be sure to smash that subscribe button!" The more actions viewers take when watching a video (and the longer they watch), the more YouTube will reward the creator in the algorithm. So even though it probably feels repetitive, make your ask at least twice in each video — once at the beginning and once at the end.

7. **Keep doing the work, not talking about the work.** At some point, creators think it's a good idea to "go meta" and start explaining how they make their videos, aiming the message at followers who are hoping to — well, *follow* — in their footsteps.

   There might be a few exceptions, but this is usually a mistake. The best creators are focused on what made them popular in the first place. Some followers might want the behind-the-scenes details, but most don't. Do the work!

The Show Goes On

Why do so many people queue up to watch Jakey Boehm try to sleep through interruptions that they pay for? Even though it seems random and absurd, I think there's a real answer.

For Boehm and others, the mass appeal comes down to a combination of three qualities: entertainment, education, and personal connection.

The ratios of these components vary among creators and are hard to quantify, but I'm convinced that these elements are critical. To make a sustainable business out of it, you also need to deliver something of value—and then find creative ways to keep up a steady stream of fresh, fun content, all while staying "on-brand."

When I last talked to Rebecca Rogers, her podcast had been purchased by a big production company. She was also scheduled to speak at eight educational conferences over the next few months.

Miss Excel had recently celebrated her two-year anniversary of making videos. In a behind-the-scenes clip, she shared the image of her old bedroom where she got started. Then she showed the keys to her dream house, where she now lived.

Over on YouTube, the Lockpicking Lawyer seemed to have no trouble finding new types of lock to pick, and every video he posted was met with more enthusiasm from subscribers. And of course, he kept gently promoting his business, where those sub-scribers could purchase more lock-picking kits of their own.

As for Jakey Boehm, the Aussie sleepfluencer, he kept livestreaming every night. He'd added a new laser show and a medley of cow sounds, all available in exchange for virtual gifts.

All of those followers needed new content to consume, and these creators were happy to give it to them.

Chapter Seven

Click Here to Paint a Masterpiece

CONCEPT: Original art of all types and styles can now be made in seconds using artificial intelligence tools. Meanwhile, you can now use similar tools to write advertising slogans, product descriptions, poetry, and more. You own whatever you create, and there are few restrictions on selling it.

The Colorado State Fair has been held in the city of Pueblo almost every year since 1872, four years before Colorado itself became a state. Its most popular features include free concerts, corn dogs on sticks, a variety of carnival games, and a number of competitions, including something called Market Hog Showmanship. But for a few days in 2022, the big news coming out of the Colorado State Fair had nothing to do with farm animals or Ferris wheels. Instead, it was about the annual fine arts competition.

The winner, Jason Allen, had entered a piece he titled *Théâtre D'opéra Spatial*. It was a beautiful image that depicted women dressed in Renaissance-era attire gazing out at a futuristic orb of light.

It was also a computer-generated image, commonly known as AI art, and Allen had "painted" it by typing a series of prompts on his keyboard.

Once the prize was announced and it was revealed that Allen had used AI, a heated debate ensued. "We're watching the death of artistry unfold right before our eyes," one commentator wrote. It was an opinion that a lot of other artists shared.

But what did Allen do wrong? He wasn't trying to pass it off as anything it wasn't. He submitted his work in the digital art category, and even tagged it "with Midjourney," crediting the service he had used to make it. It wasn't a prank. And yet the fact that an AI algorithm had produced a work of art superior (according to the judges, at least) to that of Allen's human competitors was astonishing.

The Robots ~~Are Coming~~ Have Arrived

The term *AI*, which of course stands for *artificial intelligence*, refers to computers' ability to "think" like humans through the process of machine learning. Essentially, AI algorithms apply complex mathematical calculations to recognize patterns within large sets of data. The more data AI receives, the more it "learns" to accurately label, classify, and categorize new data. Type in the right prompts, and it will draw on all those patterns to create something entirely new and different.

This technology is ever-present in our lives already, even if we don't always notice it. AI uses data on traffic patterns and inputs from cameras, sensors, and radar to power Tesla's self-driving vehicles. The AI that animates digital assistants like Alexa and Siri uses voice and search data to answer your questions and obey your demands. An AI chess engine can beat the very best human grandmasters almost every time, because it's learned the optimal move in any scenario based on data from billions of chess games.

AI, in other words, is a game changer. And it's becoming more and more sophisticated, user-friendly, and omnipresent every day.

Art in Less Than 10 Minutes: How It Works

To understand how Jason Allen had achieved this impressive feat, I signed up for Midjourney, the generator tool that he had used to win the art prize in Colorado, and started making images. Naturally, I started with cats. I present to you one of my first works in its worldwide debut:

Pencil drawing of a cat drinking a milkshake, c. 2022
Courtesy of the artist

To create this masterpiece, I first went back to school and took eighty hours of classes in composition. I then visited a cat café in search of models, where I spent another eighty hours trying to get one to pose long enough for me to capture their likeness. Just kidding! To make this image, I logged on to Midjourney and typed this sentence: *Pencil drawing of a cat drinking a milkshake.*

Thirty seconds later, the app produced an image much like the one you see here. I told it to make a few more versions until I had one I especially liked. The process was complete within five minutes.

Several popular tools (probably even more so by the time you read this) now allow anyone to create art in any style imaginable — from abstract illustrations to photorealistic paintings to watercolors and much more — for as little as $15 a month. You simply type a series of words into an interface and click submit, and seconds later, three or more versions of the image appear on-screen. From there, you can make additional variations, or tweak your request to add or remove objects or alter proportions and colors.

Alternatively, you could upload a photo and ask the AI generator to turn it into an illustration, avatar, or portrait. Thanks to AI-enabled "beauty filters," you can even ask it to create an "enhanced" version of your original photo, perhaps by brightening your eye color, smoothing out your skin tone, narrowing your jawline, and so on. Once satisfied, you can tell the generator to make high-resolution versions of your favorites.

The key point is that these AI tools aren't just searching a bunch of databases and returning with the best match they can find. That's what Google does — and compared to AI, it's old-school. Instead, the AI scans its own library of data and *uniquely builds each image you request*. All you have to do is sit back and let the robots of the future take over.

Discovering and playing around with one of these tools feels like using the internet for the first time. You're simply overwhelmed with the raw power of technology. It's exciting and more than a little scary.

As you might imagine, many artists hate the fact that anyone with the ability to type can make an unlimited amount of AI-generated art that's difficult (and sometimes impossible) to distinguish from that of a human artist. All of which begs the inevitable question: *If it's made by a computer, is it really art?*

Within the art world, that question is the subject of contentious debate. But it's not one that this book is going to resolve. This chapter is about how you can put AI tools to use for your benefit.

WHO OWNS AI ART?

Short answer: *You* most likely own whatever you create, but it's tricky. The companies behind some of the more commercial AI tools are proactive about making it clear that as far as they're concerned, creators own the work they make on the platform (a nice change from tech companies that use terms and conditions to make aggressive claims about data and IP ownership, in favor of the company).

Yet for several years, the US Copyright Office (USCO) refused to recognize copyright on AI-generated works, citing a "lack of human authorship,"* and companies such

* https://www.smithsonianmag.com/smart-news/us-copyright-office-rules -ai-art-cant-be-copyrighted-180979808.

as Getty Images have warned their contributors against using AI art.

However, this isn't a settled matter. Many experts believe that the tide will turn in favor of creators at some point. And in the meantime, you can always tweak an AI-created image using Photoshop or other editing software, thus creating a stronger copyright claim.

Did a Human Write This Book?

AI art is not confined specifically to visual mediums. You can also make AI-composed electronic music, record an audiobook narrated by AI "voiceover artists," and even have AI compose short stories or poems in the style of Emily Dickinson or Edgar Allan Poe.

In fact, when it comes to artistic expression, there's not a lot that AI *can't* do, or at least very little that won't be possible before much longer. A few years ago, for example, someone created an Eminem AI and wrote a song in the style of "feminist Eminem." Someone else used AI to compose a new *Hamilton* song, which sounds a lot like the ones Lin-Manuel Miranda wrote.

And of course there's a whole other category, best described by the so-called Rule 34 of the internet, which states that "if it exists, there's porn of it." We'll leave that topic for another book.

While learning about AI art, I also played around with a demo of one of the text generators, an AI tool that can be used to generate essays, articles, or advertising copy, all based on a short prompt. I wrote the beginnings of a sentence, *Today I went to the store,* and added the keywords *bananas* and *beer.*

Then I watched as the following words appeared on the screen as if someone were typing:

> Today I went to the store to buy some bananas. I bought one extra-large banana, wrapped in a sandwich bag and came home to eat it. The store was open a little later than my usual one and therefore I felt it would be a better option to go there today. Then I started thinking about beer. Wouldn't it be nice to have a tasty beer to go with my banana?
>
> Yep, I would like that. So here is the plan I came up with: Let me grab the extra-large banana (now wrapped in my own sandwich bag) and take it over to my friend Otto's house. Otto owns a bar near where I live. I will buy Otto's beer and stay at Otto's bar until the last banana is gone.

Okay, so if you're thinking this isn't Pulitzer Prize–winning material, you're right. But this was attempt #1. If you're not feeling the vibe in Otto's bar, or if you think it's weird to wrap bananas in a sandwich bag, you just click on an icon and try again.

This time I used the same prompt but removed the keywords. What would the app give me if I provided less direction?

Today I went to the store. I don't know about you but I can never make a grocery list and stick to it. That is why I use the following method: first I pick up any three or four items that I know I will need. So if I need cat food then I grab one of those cute round cans.

Then I put a sticker on my brain to remind me. After I've got my groceries, I put everything into the buggy. If I need toilet paper or paper towels, I just get two boxes at a time.

Then I take out all of the non-perishable items. Then I move on to my next and last pick of items. This method usually makes it to the checkout with exactly the amount of items on the list.

I do have a small issue with our town grocery store but I am trying to get over that (that story is for another day).

Again, not perfect. A sticker on my brain? Is a buggy some form of shopping cart? Not to mention the fact that the robot really left me hanging about the issue with the town grocery store.

Still, the fact that text like this can be summoned at will from a few initial keystrokes is impressive. Just as with visual art, these paragraphs aren't being pulled from a database somewhere.

They're being created in real time. Reusing the same prompt will result in a different outcome.

But while it's cool to experiment with the AI writing programs, they do have limits. For example, I couldn't get them to write this book for me (though I tried!). A passable snippet of Shakespeare or a poem that sounds exactly like Emily Dickinson is one thing, but creating a complete, coherent work that stays on topic for more than a paragraph or two is quite another.

As I was writing this chapter, the research lab OpenAI announced a new version of its language-learning model: their latest and much more sophisticated iteration of the same kind of tool I'd used to generate a short story about going to the store. Yes, I'm talking about ChatGPT, the chatbot that took the internet by storm.

I decided to try again with this hyped-up new tool to see if the ChatGPT version was really so much better. Specifically, I asked it to "Write a short story about a fictional bar named for its owner, Otto. The story should involve beer and bananas, and end with a moral."

As you'll see in a moment, I got exactly what I asked for. This time, it didn't feel as much like it was written by a robot, even though obviously it was.

Granted, the moral at the end was a little basic ("sometimes it pays to be open-minded"), and the story wasn't filled with page-turning drama, but that could have been my fault. Maybe I should have added "page-turning drama" to the prompt!

Nevertheless, as someone who writes for a living, I suddenly understood how painters, photographers, and other visual artists feel when exploring AI art. *This is incredible,* I thought. *And also terrifying.*

Otto's Bar

not written by the author

Otto's Bar was a popular hangout in the small town of Millville, known for its cheap drinks and laid-back atmosphere. Otto, the owner, was a friendly and jovial man who loved nothing more than chatting with his customers and pouring them a cold one.

One hot summer evening, a group of friends stopped by Otto's for a round of beers. As they were chatting and laughing at the bar, a young woman walked in carrying a large bunch of bananas.

"What can I do for you, miss?" Otto asked, eyeing the bananas curiously.

"I heard that you have the best beer in town," the woman replied. "I was hoping to trade these bananas for a few bottles."

Otto was a bit taken aback, but he couldn't help but be intrigued. He had never traded beer for bananas before.

"Well, I suppose I could give you a bottle or two for those bananas," Otto said with a chuckle. "But I have to warn you, my beer is worth a lot more than a bunch of fruit."

The woman smiled. "I understand, but I assure you, these bananas are special. They were grown on a small farm in a distant land and are said to have magical properties."

Otto was skeptical, but he was also a bit of a risk taker. He figured he had nothing to lose and agreed to the trade. He gave the woman two bottles of his finest beer in exchange for the bananas.

As it turned out, the bananas were indeed special. After eating just one, the group of friends at the bar noticed that they were suddenly more energized and alert. They finished their beers in record time and even played a few rounds of pool before heading home.

The moral of the story is that sometimes it pays to be open-minded and take a chance on something new. You never know what opportunities might come your way.

Enough About Bots — Let's Talk About Making Money

Angus Russell was living in Sydney, Australia when a friend commented on his interior design aesthetic. It was, to put it charitably, sparse. Since Russell had nothing on his walls, his friend suggested he hang some artwork.

The next day, Russell went online and tried to find some cool paintings, but nothing he saw was quite right. Plus, art was expensive! He started to wonder if there was some way to pay less money for custom-made art that he really loved. That's when it hit him: he'd heard of AI art, which was still in its infancy at the time, and he wondered if he could use it to put his *own* artwork on the walls. It turned out that he could. Then he wondered if this might be something that other people would want to do as well.

Russell launched NightCafe Studio via a Reddit post in November 2019. Named for a painting by Vincent van Gogh, the site's AI-driven NightCafe Creator tool allows users to easily create their own digital art, then immediately order it in poster form.

Since its inception, NightCafe has been used to generate more than five million unique works of art. It now has five full-time employees and brings in more than $1 million a year in recurring revenue.

Most people use NightCafe to make art to hang on their own walls. But you can just as easily—and perhaps more profitably—make art for other people to buy. Companies offering print-on-demand (POD) services enable anyone to create a virtual shop where customers can browse, see how the artwork will look on a range of materials, and buy it.

Print-on-demand can be more than just posters. Most companies that provide the service will also print custom art on anything from T-shirts to throw pillows. The list of products also includes sports bras, yoga pants, mouse pads, beanbags, jigsaw puzzles, and trucker hats.

If you can find someone who wants your AI-generated art on their sports bra or trucker hat (or both!), POD providers will manufacture and ship it to them. The most popular POD companies, like Printful and Printly, offer integrations with Shopify, WordPress, and other e-commerce platforms to make it easy to set up an online shop in an hour or less. All you need is buyers, and to make that part easier, these e-commerce platforms often integrate with creator platforms such as Instagram and TikTok. Just share your designs and point your followers to your shop!

AI art is yet another example of how technology has enabled an explosion in microentrepreneurship within just the last few years. It wasn't long ago that I wrote about how amateur photographers could earn some cash by creating a library of stock photos and making them available for sale. The only catch was that this process required them to, you know, go out and take photographs, then edit each one individually before posting it.

Now, of course, it's much simpler, weirder, and faster. Instead of having to go out into the wild to find the perfect photo op, anyone can simply type in a few keywords from the comfort of their couch and achieve the same result. As one digital artist on YouTube put it: "I used to spend hours upon hours making graphic elements. Now I spend minutes on them, and they look just as good."

How much art is now AI-generated? It's hard to say, but one thing's for sure: you can expect this technology—and the ways in which it can be applied—to grow by leaps and bounds going forward.

In the near future, entire podcasts will be written and voiced by AI. Musicians and DJs will publish songs written (and in some cases *performed*) by AI. Publishing companies will release works of fiction and collections of poetry written by AI. Visual artists will build careers exclusively through AI art. Some of them will disclose their process and others won't, and scandals will ensue when the artists who don't are found out.

One thing is for sure: this particular revolution will be algorithmically digitized.

GRAPHIC NOVEL IN A DAY

In a twenty-minute video tutorial, an artist with the moniker PhilFTW demonstrated how to use AI art to create an entire graphic novel in less than a day. It seems incredible, but it's true.

The artist's real name is Alex Colvin and he'd spent twenty years working in corporate advertising before leaving to work at an indie game studio. When he first started experimenting with AI-generated comics, it was for the sake of the art, not the money. But pretty soon Colvin realized that he might be onto something. He listed his first two comic books on Amazon's Kindle Direct Publishing platform, then prepared to create a whole anthology. In an email, he described the change as long overdue: "I work more and the pay is less, but I never feel shitty at the end of the day."*

After exploring Midjourney and a few other tools, he had an idea: Could he make his own comic book entirely with AI?

It got better: Not only could he show people how to make original comic books, he promised, but he could show them how to do the whole thing in just a day. The steps involved would take a few hours to do properly, but still—the pace and the quality you can get from these tools are amazing.

To try it yourself, follow these steps:

1. Source a broad series of related images from an AI art generator. You want to make a wide range, but you also want them to look like they belong next to each other. (You'll get better at this as you start creating images.)

---

* He also said: "I wish I would have figured this out a decade earlier but I feel fortunate to be forty-two and living the dream. Too many people don't know they have the option."

2. Write the "story" for the comic using an AI text generator. As with visual art, where finding the perfect images requires iteration, you'll likely get lots of throwaway text for every usable paragraph. Discard what you don't need and keep the rest.

3. Edit the story into short chunks of text that contain a single idea or line of dialogue. These snippets will be used as captions to accompany your images.

4. Using Photoshop or other design software, lay out the images and text for each page. For your first comic, something like eight to twelve pages is ideal.

5. Create and add a cover (using AI art, naturally!) to your layout.

6. There is no step six — you just made a graphic novel! What you do with it next is up to you.

How to Paint Fake Picassos

There are many different ways to make AI art, but they all require an AI art generator.

Luckily, most are free or cheap to use. For my $30-a-month "pro" subscription to Midjourney, I could make an unlimited number of cats drinking milkshakes — or of course, anything else I wanted. Some apps are completely free, though they tend to have more limited features or require more programming skill than the ones you pay for.

According to one online tutorial, learning to use these tools generally occurs in four stages. In level one, you're just beginning to experiment. This is described as the stage at which you might exclaim, "Oh my God, I just typed in a sentence and made a beautiful image!"

I laughed in recognition of that experience.

Level two is where you realize that getting an online engine to replicate what's in your head is a lot more difficult than it seems. And levels three and four are where you become increasingly skilled at summoning these initial images and improving them at increasingly precise levels of detail.

Here are some tips on how to get there.

Get better at prompts. Being able to use and manipulate AI art tools is a skill. It's not quite coding, and not quite design or photography, but it draws on elements of each.

Even though these tools aren't complicated to use, a little knowledge goes a long way. One way to get better at generating images is by studying the frequently used prompts that make it to the top of the community Discord or "featured" page. Try playing around with these common prompts by adding or subtracting phrases. The more you do it, the easier it will be to write original prompts of your own.

Prompts typically take on an intuitive language structure that begins with the desired subject, followed by any parameters or additional details, and ends with any photography or illustration specs (like what styles you like) and an aspect ratio (your desired ratio of height to width). For example, to create a landscape portrait, you'd type something like this:

landscape, temple in background, 16:9

That's a simple version. It might produce something interesting, but you'll get better results by getting more detailed. To soup up your prompt, type something like this:

Burmese landscape at sunset in the style of Ansel Adams, temple in background, majestic, detailed, lots of light, 4k, 16:9

There are many videos and online tutorials that explain this process in detail. Though I'll never be on par with the users who can summon realistic anime characters with a few keystrokes, I was able to improve my basic skills within a couple of hours just by playing around.

Create a signature style of your own. AI tools are excellent at replicating the style of famous artists. But anyone can use these tools to create a painting that looks like a Picasso—which means that if you want your work to stand out, you'll need a style of your own.

Pay attention, because this is where the real expertise comes in. Specializing in certain themes or types of images will set you apart from the amateurs—which may come in handy when you're trying to sell your art through print-on-demand.

Make a bunch of variations. Once you get some practice, get to work making lots of variations on a single idea.

Having some traditional photo-editing skills can come in handy here, because while AI art is amazing, it doesn't always give you exactly what you want. So if you're able to tweak your creations somewhat—by adding text, cropping parts of the image, or merging images, for example—chances are they'll be a lot more attractive to potential buyers. Which brings us to...

How to Sell Your Masterpieces

Set up an online shop. Angus Russell benefited from his Night-Cafe business's being one of the first to let users not only generate images, but also print physical replicas to hang on their wall. It was a smart move—but now that this market has grown, you'll do better by finding a specific niche to focus on.

Shopify and other all-in-one merchant platforms make it fairly easy to set up your own shop, complete with your own domain name and custom logo. Typically, you'll make an account on one of those platforms, integrating it with a company that specializes in print-on-demand.

If you have experience setting up a blog or basic website, you'll be up and running in a couple of hours. If you haven't done anything like that before, it may take a bit longer.

For an even simpler setup, you can simply register with a company like Redbubble, which does everything in one place but doesn't allow you nearly as much customization. You could test the waters there first and see how it feels.

"Stage" your work. If you're selling physical versions of your digital art, get high-quality photos of it looking good in a nice home or office. Even though most platforms will automatically include images showing how your art might look on someone's wall, your shop will seem more legit if you go a bit further. Order framed samples of some of your best work and take nice photos of them hanging in your home or office. If needed, ask a friend for help, either with staging them in a better location, or with the photography if that's not in your skill set.

Create an Instagram profile and start posting images. Once you have a shop, you need buyers. Instagram has its problems, and it doesn't work for every kind of business—but for something like this, it's ideal. Set up a new profile devoted exclusively to your new art. Follow the classic rules of "social media management": post every day, use relevant hashtags, follow and like the posts of industry leaders, and engage with your followers.

Include a link to the shop in your profile, and make it clear in every post that followers can purchase prints of anything they'd like. You can also sell them through Amazon or Etsy, or even set up multiple shops with distinct identities on each of these platforms. One artist on YouTube says he earns $5,000 a month selling his AI creations this way. The print-on-demand apps seem designed for this, with several of them offering the ability to run "up to ten shops" on the pro-level plan.

———

As powerful as AI is, making consistent, high-quality AI art requires effort. I had fun learning to write prompts, but I wasn't going to win any fine art competitions. Most of my attempts at depicting ninja cats in feudal Japan, for example, failed to launch. Similarly, while I enjoyed my brief stint as a short-story writer, those AI-generated stories aren't winning any literary awards, either—at least for the moment.

Still, these AI tools can be used to speed up an existing process, allowing artists, writers, and other creatives to save time while developing their valuable skills; to dramatically expand the volume and variety of digital products they produce and sell, or to outsource the rote and repetitive parts of the artistic process, freeing up humans to focus their energy on the more creative stuff.

While the singularity (where artificial intelligence surpasses human intelligence and starts to take over) hasn't arrived yet, AI *is* getting more and more powerful all the time. These tools can be used for fun (cats drinking milkshakes; short stories about shopping), for making money (selling your Picasso-inspired works), or both.

There will always be computers, and there will always be humans. Just don't think you'll always be able to tell the difference between their work.

Chapter Eight
The Human IPO

CONCEPT: Need money for a business idea? You can now get funding from direct investors without going through gatekeepers. You can also become a manager of your own fund, overseeing a Shark Tank–*like operation that spends other people's money.*

In the spring of 2020, Alex Masmej was broke. He lived in Paris but wanted to relocate to San Francisco—a city not exactly known for its affordable cost of living. He could have gotten a job at Starbucks, picked up some freelancing gigs, or spent his weekends shuttling passengers around in an Uber, but it would have taken him many months to raise the cash he needed. Instead, Alex filed what he called a "human IPO" to fund the move. He created a digital token ($ALEX) and announced to his network that he was seeking $20,000 in return for 10 percent of the income he would generate over the following three years.

Alex got the money, but he also got something even more valuable. His idea was so novel, and so brilliant in its simplicity, that it attracted attention from many of the people he hoped to meet in San Francisco—his whole reason for moving there in the first place—which in turn led to a number of opportunities.

There was only one part of the plan that didn't quite work out as expected: Alex had originally wanted to get a job at a start-up, but he ended up founding his own company instead.

Sell Your Future

It used to be that if you had an idea, as well as a plan for how to build, monetize, and scale a business around that idea (all detailed and colorfully graphed in your thirty-slide pitch deck), a bank or venture capital firm might give you money for it—in exchange for a portion of equity or future earnings, of course.

Now, however, groups of microinvestors are offering infusions of capital to individuals with the mere glimmer of a plan for a company. In some cases, the individuals just have *ideas*. Sometimes they simply demonstrate enough talent or charisma, and give off the vibe of someone sure to have game-changing ideas in the future.

In short, finding someone to invest in you has never been easier. How do you do that? For one answer, don't focus on finding the idea that people will want to invest in at some point in the future. Instead, focus on finding the people who already want to invest in *your* future.

The idea of a "human IPO" may seem strange. But is it really? After all, most forms of investing involve buying a share in a company's future earnings—so why wouldn't there be investors out there interested in buying part of a *person's* future earnings?

Jason Zook, who once got paid to wear a different brand's T-shirt every day for four years, thought it was possible. Being a human billboard was a cool trick that paid well, but eventually Jason got sick of the "I Wear Your Shirt" business and decided to double down with a unique offer to his followers.

He'd been working on a bunch of online courses and coaching programs, and in addition to signing up for any particular offering, his followers could also pay $1,000 for access to *anything he would make in the future*. Fittingly, he called it "Buy My Future"—and he earned $178,000 from it. Two years later, he repeated the process with his wife ("Buy Our Future") and brought in another $300,000.

A Brief History of Business Investing

If you've followed the explosion of start-ups coming out of places like Silicon Valley, you'd be forgiven for thinking that money falls from the sky—or from the money fairies in the government, who print whatever they want.

Historically speaking, however, the money used to start new businesses more often came from groups of financiers. As far back as the eighteenth century, this model was used to fund whaling ships that ventured out into arctic waters. These were costly expeditions that could deliver a large profit, provided the ships returned with valuable whale oil and other goods.

Sometimes, however, the ships were lost at sea, literally sinking all that investment capital. Investors soon figured out that they could diversify their investment and therefore minimize their risk by financing multiple ships, captains, and voyages.

The biggest investors were cartels like the East India Company: quasi-governmental organizations that funded colonialism as well as whaling expeditions. The cartels eventually became so powerful that they were able to dictate the terms of these agreements, which meant that they grew richer by the minute while trampling on anyone in their way.*

It was unfair on every level, and enough to turn your ordinary business owner into a follower of Karl Marx, who chronicled the corrupt history of the East India Company in his regular newspaper columns.

Eventually, the government-funded cartels morphed into banks and other financial institutions. For another century or two, if you needed capital, you went to the banks with your hat in hand.

---

* Including: most of India and Pakistan, parts of China, and several Indonesian islands.

In the run-up to the first dot-com boom, the balance of power shifted once again as venture capitalists began to drive the start-up world. Now, instead of taking a note that promised repayment with interest, investors were trading their capital for a share in the company itself. What's more, thanks to globalization and technology, the cost to start many businesses went way down.

Beginning in the Web2 era, platforms launched with the promise of making direct investment easier. A big one was Kiva, founded in 2005 with the mission to support "microgrants" to individuals in poor countries. Thanks to a network of in-country organizations operating in partnership with Kiva, anyone could go online and peruse listings for thousands of entrepreneurial projects. They could then loan $50,000 or less to any project, most of which was eventually repaid.*

Crowdfunding took off in 2007–2010, when three major platforms debuted. One was Kickstarter, whose stated mission is to help bring creative projects to life. Another was Indiegogo, which originally focused on raising money for independent films before expanding into all kinds of entrepreneurial projects. The third was GoFundMe, which allows people to invest in virtually any project or cause under the sun.

Now, instead of small loans, ordinary investors could

---

* More than two million lenders have used Kiva, and the organization boasts a repayment rate of 96 percent.

contribute as little as $10 toward the fundraising goal for any given project. If the goal was met, they would receive a reward, usually in the form of the product or service they helped to finance.

Patreon emerged a few years later, with the goal of allowing fans to financially support musicians and artists directly. Crucially, Patreon was structured around *recurring* donations, not just one-time fundraising campaigns. This provided many artists with a consistent source of income, enabling them to earn a reliable living through their work.

As life-changing as they are for those who use them, however, these platforms each had their niche. Kiva connects lenders with microborrowers in poor countries. Kickstarter is about *projects*, and tends to perform best with projects involving a physical item that needs to be manufactured (a board game, a gadget, etc.). Most successful Patreon campaigns are for artists, writers, or musicians. But none was quite right for everyone else.

Instead of crowdfunding, many of those who sought outside investment for larger projects usually followed a "lean start-up" philosophy of raising money through venture capital. The only catch was, they needed gatekeepers to make introductions or act as sherpas to guide them through the process. Like most things in a capitalist economy, it worked well for some and didn't work at all for many others.

Contrary to how it's portrayed through popular TV shows like *Shark Tank*, where founders compete for approval and investment from rich entrepreneurs, this system is frustratingly opaque. *Shark Tank* is entertaining, even inspiring, but everyone involved—including the Sharks—is in it for the PR. Most filmed segments are never aired. Most deals that are struck are never finalized. That's okay, because again...it's less about raising capital to fund an idea than it is about the PR.

A friend who went on *Dragons' Den,* the Canadian version of *Shark Tank,* told me up front that she had zero desire to actually get funded. Given the limitations of these existing models, she simply wanted the millions of people watching to hear about her tea brand.

Peer-to-Peer Payments Are the Norm

One thing that's helped fuel this rise in private fundraising efforts is the simple fact that exchanging money is different than it used to be. Peer-to-peer payments through apps like Venmo, Zelle, and Cash App are the default mode for many young people, cutting out the middleman of banks and credit card companies. It's fast, easy, and decentralized—or at least, *less centralized* than ever before.

Some of this was accelerated by the pandemic, when the rise in online and "contactless" purchasing drove more and more people toward digital payment methods, but the trend was already well underway.

These days, it seems like any and everyone is accepting peer-to-peer payments, and in fact, many prefer it. Everyone from therapists to pet groomers to supermarkets is now happily accepting these types of payments. At some point my hairdresser began asking for Venmo instead of my credit card ("because of taxes"). Using an app called OfferUp, I found a guy named Nick who earns most of his income selling plants. Plant Guy Nick, as I call him, accepts *only* Venmo or Cash App for payment.*

For another example of how people are pursuing even more direct means of funding., let's turn to the podcasting world.

YOUR KICKSTARTER SUCKS
(BUT IS ALSO KIND OF AWESOME)

Because it's the internet, there's also an absurd side to crowdfunding. The podcast *Your Kickstarter Sucks* highlights some of the most bizarre campaigns, some of which managed to actually attract funding.

Between browsing the show's archives and some online research of my own, here are a few campaigns I thought were particularly notable.

---

* PayPal went from being the preferred method of payment for many businesses to being ostracized for its take-no-prisoners approach to data sharing and arbitrarily closing accounts. Even the founders, Elon Musk and Peter Thiel, have distanced themselves from it.

- A rapper known as B.o.B., who attempted to raise $200,000 in a campaign to prove that the earth was flat. Alas, the campaign itself fell flat, raising only $650.

- A minimalist Nativity set—it was a Kickstarter staff pick!—that consisted of figurines in the form of plain wooden blocks. "It is up to you to interpret the set," the creator wrote. "I find the variations quite fascinating."

- Have you ever wanted to lick your cat? Now you can. Advertised as a "novel and fun way to bond with your cat," this grooming brush will allow you to "lick your cat clean but without the furballs," according to a promise from the creators of LICKI brush. It raised $52,179.

- A "Booze/Drugs/Cigs" GoFundMe page started by an enterprising student who reported being "Broke af and trynna have a lit summer."

- An app that would allow users to "download" energy from the air, converting it into a usable power source. Sounds amazing! And also, impossible. IndieGoGo shut it down. :(

- A Swedish designer who created a concept for a "multi service bed robot." The Bed Botixs could make the bed, for example, or wake you up by gently

nudging you if you failed to respond to the alarm.
But that's not all! It could also provide massage on
demand, and even help out with intimate acts. Tragi-
cally, the Bed Botixs never came to life.

Shameless Acquisition Target

Laura Mayer has a claim to fame: as far as she can tell, she's the
person responsible for producing more hit podcasts than anyone
else in the industry. Popular shows she's helped launch include
Malcolm Gladwell's *Revisionist History, Happier with Gretchen
Rubin,* and *Bad Blood*—just to name a few. She can now add
another achievement to her résumé: that of starting her own
show on the topic of getting a podcast acquired.

Laura was employee number one at Panoply, a podcast production studio that grew by leaps and bounds in its first few
years, during which she worked around the clock to turn the
company into one of the top destinations for podcasting talent.

To achieve this, she gave Panoply her all, which turned out to
be too much. Once, she called into a meeting from the hospital.
Even after her bosses learned of her location, she was still chas-
tised for not showing up in person.

When she finally quit to work for a competing start-up, her
employer rewarded her years of service by taking away all of

her phantom equity. Three years later, the company was sold for $200 million. Laura, of course, got nothing.

At the time, she was living in an expensive part of Brooklyn with her husband and their young daughter, and wanted to be able to buy a home. But of course she couldn't afford it, having missed out on all those stock options. What could she do?

The answer came in the form of—what else?—a new podcast.

She launched her own show with an intentionally unsubtle title. It was called *Shameless Acquisition Target.*

In this show, Laura promised to offer a behind-the-scenes look at the inner workings of the podcast world. It wasn't just an exposé, though—it was a proof of concept for a whole new business model.

How to Fish for Sharks

Laura's show came in the wake of a time when podcast networks—like the one she had run for three years—were hungry for content and buying up podcast properties left and right. Gimlet Media sold to Spotify for $230 million. Another network was acquired for $120 million. Almost every month, another big deal was announced.

Laura wanted her show to be acquired, too (hence the name, which left no room for ambiguity), and set a six-week deadline to receive offers.

The campaign she produced for *Shameless Acquisition Target* was playful in its audacity. The tagline was "the show that sells itself." The opening theme song, which she commissioned from a musician on Fiverr, referenced her goal of making "house money." A teaser episode asked, "Will she make hundreds, millions, or even dozens of dollars?"

As a way of filling out the human side of the story, she recorded her conversations with her husband as they walked around a mystery house in the neighborhood that Laura desperately wanted to be able to afford. The house became a minor character in the narrative itself, leading Laura to sell branded T-shirts with a picture of it (technically, it was a similar-looking house, since she worried about getting sued by the people who actually owned it). Though their projects were quite different, Alex Masmej and Laura Mayer followed a similar process for finding the right "shark" to fund it.

They started with a "shot across the bow"—publishing an idea in the hope that it would find the right investor. It was important that the idea be interesting and novel, but Alex and Laura both knew that merely releasing something weird into the world wasn't enough to get it discovered. So in addition to announcing their projects publicly, even more work took place privately as they reached out to friends of friends behind the scenes, working every available angle that might lead to funding.

It was a three-part process: the deal post, the warm outreach, and the cold pitch.

1. The Deal Post

A deal post is essentially an announcement of your funding request, and can take many forms. For Alex, it was very simple: it started with a series of tweets, as well as a talk he gave at a crypto event in Paris. For Laura, it was much more complex, since her podcast was both the deal post and the product itself. Still, the two-minute trailer for her podcast served as the most basic entry point for someone to learn about it.

Even if you're primarily using social media for your announcement, I recommend that you also create a written version on a website or blog post. It's just helpful to have something else to point to. Whatever you choose, it's important to have a place to send people who want to learn more about you.

2. The Warm Outreach

Once you have a deal post ready to go, you'll want to make sure your friends, colleagues, and acquaintances know about it. I call this *the warm outreach* because it's different from pitching a stranger. The more influencers (like, actual ones—meaning people who can connect you to investors, not just people with lots of random followers) you can connect with at this stage, the better.

While every project is different, for many creators the warm outreach is more important than the cold pitch. It's during this time that you'll connect with potential ambassadors who can help many other people learn about it.

Even though I'd known Laura Mayer for a number of years by the time she launched her podcast, we hadn't kept in touch well and I probably would have missed the news about her project if she hadn't reached out to her circle to announce it.

But I didn't hear about it from her directly. She wrote to the editor of *Hot Pod*, a popular newsletter for podcast insiders. That's where Jonathan Fields, a longtime friend, heard about it, then listened to the first episode and mentioned it to me. Then I saw that Gretchen Rubin, another friend, had also mentioned it in her newsletter.

With both Jonathan and Gretchen providing recommendations, I streamed the trailer and loved it. From there, I subscribed and listened to the whole series. That's the power of a network in action.

3. The Cold Pitch

If you're very lucky, you may attract exactly the right investor(s) through the public deal post and warm outreach. Often, however, you'll need to go wider, and reach out to people you don't currently know.

It helps to develop a "hit list" of potential investors, perhaps starting from online VC directories (Crunchbase has one, for example) or by using Twitter to search for recent mentions of *AngelList, venture capital,* or similar. Just be sure to do some further research, of course, since many of those mentions won't lead to the kind of people you want to target—but some will, so your goal is to find the diamonds.

When you're cold pitching, a few rules apply. First, lower your expectations. Be grateful if you hear back from anyone at all, and be gracious no matter what. Keep your introductory communication short and to the point. You're just looking for a foot in the door.

If people express interest, send them the link to the deal post, but don't oversell it—you want your project to largely speak for itself, and you don't want to seem desperate. If you have a slide deck, ask if it's okay to send it before doing so.

Most VCs and other active investors get *a lot* of unwanted pitches. But this doesn't mean you should give up on getting noticed. Like the literary agent who dreams of finding the next great American novel in a pile of rejects, most of them are still looking for those hidden gems. They don't just want the next big thing, they want the next *potentially* big thing that no one else has. It's your job to help them find it.

One more thing: Your recruitment efforts have much higher odds of success if there's some sort of built-in urgency. You don't want a potential investor to think *This looks interesting,* then file it away. You want them to think *I'd better jump on this NOW.*

Otherwise, you run the risk of being lost in the shuffle of constant information flow.

Laura did this in her *Shameless Acquisition Target* podcast by introducing a deadline. With each week's episode, she challenged sponsors to exceed the amount of funding that the previous week's sponsor had provided. Then, toward the end, the show went dark for thirty days. During that time, she told the audience she'd entertain pitches before announcing a decision in the next episode.

So what happened in the end? Several things. The first was that her work on *Shameless* attracted a compelling new job offer. It wasn't what she'd had in mind when she started the project, but as much fun as she'd had experimenting with this new fundraising model she'd invented, along the way she'd realized she might be better suited for the world of traditional work after all, at least while her daughter was young.

The second was that she connected with a literary agent and began turning the idea into a book proposal, with film and TV rights also in the works. I wouldn't be surprised if Laura Mayer ends up with that house after all.

The Gatekeepers Have Left the Building

Today, a new ecosystem of decentralized microinvesting platforms like AngelList and FundersClub make funding easier to obtain than ever. Not only do these platforms allow you to connect directly with investors who might want to back your project, they also make it easier to qualify for funding.

By going this route, you get to bypass the gatekeepers, which means no big institution scrutinizing your business plan and combing through your financial statements before deciding whether or not you are worthy of funding. All you need is one direct investor, somewhere, to believe in your idea.

Better yet, on these platforms, it's the users who make the rules—including the one that allows you to accept investors on a recurring basis, meaning you don't have to raise all the money you need at once. They typically do so through two primary tools, syndicates and rolling funds.

- Syndicate = a group of investors who pool their money to invest in specific companies or projects.
- Rolling fund = a single fund that offers investors the chance to invest in lots of companies or projects.

In a syndicate, each individual investor can pick and choose which companies to invest in, on a deal-by-deal basis. For a rolling fund, the fund manager makes the picks. So while investors don't get to select the companies, each rolling fund exists only for one calendar quarter, at which point investors have the option of either withdrawing their money or rolling it over into a new fund. (There are other variations on this structure, but this is the most common.)

Personal Shark Tank

Then there's the other option that microfinance has enabled: managing a rolling fund of your own. In this role, *you're* the shark, doling out investments from a portfolio of assets you control. And on platforms like AngelList, it takes only a couple of clicks to get started.

Why would you do this? Because it's cool to have your own VC firm! Oh, and also because you get to keep a percentage of the overall investment. The amount can vary (it's up to you to decide when you set up the fund), but typical management fees are around 2 percent, paid quarterly, regardless of performance.

In addition, your fund takes a cut of the profits, often in the neighborhood of *20* percent. Other administrative fees are common as well.*

To take a rough calculation, imagine you run a small fund of $1 million. Every quarter, you'd receive a management fee of $5,000, for a total of $20,000 a year. Then you get your share of the profits, also paid quarterly. If your fund earns an annualized 15 percent interest, that nets you $30,000.

---

* "Wow, that's a lot of fees!" Yes, but this is not index fund investing. You could start one of those if you prefer, but a) you'd have a hard time competing with existing companies, and b) your commissions would be much lower.

Capital: $1 million

Management fee (2 percent): $20,000/year

Performance fee (20 percent of profits, based on
   15 percent annual returns): $30,000

—

Total return: $50,000

At this point you might be wondering where on earth you're going to get that initial $1 million from.

Fair question. Of course, you can invite friends, family, and social media followers to invest in your personal *Shark Tank* operation. But in addition to whatever door-knocking you do, your fund also will be listed in a directory that investors peruse in search of their next opportunity.

Investors who come to AngelList are required to be "accredited," which is a fancy way of saying they need to have a lot of money.* Most of them are there because they want to diversify from traditional investments, so they tend to spread their bets across a lot of projects instead of looking for one big win.

A few examples of rolling funds seeking investors:

 • Climate Avengers: a team focused on supporting start-ups in sustainability.

---

* Typically, to be accredited requires a net worth of $1 million or more, not counting a primary residence, or an earned income of at least $200,000 a year.

- Region Cuatro: founded by an engineering manager at Airbnb and focusing on tech in Latin America.
- Chasing Rainbows: investing in companies led by under-represented LGTBQ+ founders.
- Unpopular Ventures Fund: focused on "the best companies off the beaten path."

You might notice something in these examples: each of the funds is designed to attract either investors who are interested in a certain sector, or investors whose values are mutually aligned (or both). In addition to themed funds like these, there are also plenty of funds with a more general focus.

Basically, if you have an idea, you can start a fund of your own. Finding the companies to invest it in is no small project. But for someone who already knows where they want to invest and is good at lining up investors, this could be an ideal option.

The Smart Money Is on the Creators

As the postpandemic economy steamrolled along, an interesting belief set in among the investor class: "It's harder to find good things to invest in than it is to get someone to give you money."

During a bull market, money always sloshes around. But even during bear markets, people are still investing. "The dumb money goes away," one founder told me. "But the smart money is always there."

In an environment like this, creators have all the power, and can benefit from the right idea even more than investors.

Of course, not every crowdfunded project will succeed, and sometimes entire syndicates or rolling funds fizzle out. Still, this model will likely evolve and grow, so expect to see new networks and platforms spring up that make agreements like these even more frictionless. Small investors will be able to tie their future returns to creative people, and the creative people with ideas will be able to raise funds to get their projects off the ground.

All of this money is going to someone. Why shouldn't it be you?

Chapter Nine

Scam the Scammers

CONCEPT: From overpriced ink cartridges to sports betting, what you've long suspected is true: The game is rigged. Companies will do anything to maintain an unfair advantage, and the government will help them out along the way.

Jeremy O'Sullivan and Melissa Nelson had hit upon a promising business idea: a service that helps McDonald's franchise owners fix their finicky ice cream machines. It all began when they noticed that the machines were programmed to be needlessly complicated and prone to malfunction, a practice that benefited the McDonald's Corporation at the expense of its franchisees, who are responsible for paying for the costly repairs and maintenance on the machines. This wasn't just an occasional problem; the popular machines were so often out of service that an app, appropriately called McBroken, sprang up to track the status of the machines at McDonald's locations worldwide.*

Where McFlurry lovers the world over saw only disappointment, O'Sullivan and Nelson, who had invented an automatic frozen yogurt dispenser called the Frobot almost a decade before, saw an opportunity to make soft serve great again. So they started a lucrative business showing franchisees how to hack the machines via an add-on gadget that kept the machines operating consistently and reduced the need for repairs.

It might sound like a win-win proposition, but instead of encouraging this development, McDonald's tried to shut it down by driving O'Sullivan and Nelson out of business, simultaneously disparaging the couple's technology and attempting to duplicate it for their own use. Executives threatened to void warranties on their own franchisees' machines if they didn't use the official vendor. Meanwhile, they claimed never to have accessed the proprietary systems that O'Sullivan and Nelson had built, even though server logs and other evidence clearly proved otherwise.

In short, it was the classic David and Goliath tale, and O'Sullivan and Nelson aren't backing down. They're fighting back with litigation and a full-court PR press to challenge the company.

McDonald's has a history of giving partners and customers less

---

* Until the lawyers shut it down, visit mcbroken.com to see for yourself whether your local McDonald's soft serve is currently available.

than promised, dating back to 1987 with the birth of the company's Monopoly promotion. Based on the popular board game, the promotion offered game pieces that could later be redeemed for prizes with each purchase. Most pieces weren't worth much, but some were valuable. A few lucky customers might receive a piece that was *very* valuable, and could be redeemed for things like a new car or a cash prize of up to $1 million.

It drove hundreds of thousands of customers to eat at McDonald's restaurants more often, in the hope of being served up one of the rare pieces that could be redeemed for much more than a Happy Meal or a milkshake. Ecstatic winners were routinely featured on local news, providing free publicity for the company.

Unfortunately, it was all a scam. The McDonald's Monopoly promotion was rigged almost from the beginning, all due to a stunningly poor hiring decision.

In classic outsourcing fashion, McDonald's had made the choice to hire a subcontractor to administer the prizes. The subcontracting company, in turn, hired a former police officer named Jerome P. Jacobson as chief of security, tasked with overseeing the contest.

Over the next fifteen years (yep), more than $13 million in winnings was diverted to individuals chosen by Jacobson. While low-value prizes continued to be distributed randomly, nearly all of the top-value prizes went to his friends, family, and coconspirators, in exchange for a cut of the earnings. This meant that no matter how many Big Macs you bought, if you weren't an associate of Jacobson's you weren't going to win the more valuable prizes. Meanwhile, Jacobson's associates netted $24 million, or about $60 million in today's dollars.

At some point the mob got involved in helping Jacobson run the scam, widening the circle of potential "winners" and drawing attention away from Jacobson.

It finally came to an end when someone talked. The FBI opened an investigation—yes, white vans and wiretaps were involved—and eventually arrested Jacobson and his henchmen.

By the time the saga came to an end, fifty-three people were indicted. Jacobson was sentenced to prison for three years.

Stories like these are more common that you'd think. And for every story of corporate malfeasance that makes headlines, as the Monopoly affair did, there are countless other cases that manage to fly under the radar. While these can range anywhere from questionable marketing practices to outright fraud, one thing is clear: more often than not, the game is rigged.

The good news is that more and more people are finding ways to fight back.

The Grandma Who Took On "Big Printer"

You could argue that the lottery drama wasn't McDonald's fault, at least not directly. After all, it was the subcontractor that made the bad decision to hire a corrupt security chief, and that was lax in its oversight. And in the end, it wasn't America's favorite fast-food chain that had committed fraud, it was the subcontractor's security director.

For Hewlett Packard, the multinational information technology company and maker of computers and printers, it was another story. When it comes to their printer line, HP follows a loss-leader strategy of selling the printers at the lowest price possible and attempting to make up for those thin profit margins on the recurring sales of overpriced ink cartridges and toner. It's the classic razor industry model, where the razor is cheap but you have to keep buying blades forever.

There was just one problem: the high price tag on the ink cartridges opened up new opportunities for other companies to make discount ink cartridges and toner that could be used in HP printers. Since HP makes most of its money on name-brand ink, it needs to keep those prices high to remain profitable, which means that after-market brands are able to sell their versions for less and still profit. (The ink itself is exactly the same—there's no reason to buy the name-brand version, unless you just like giving HP more money.)

Not surprisingly, HP wasn't very happy about this. For years the company did everything it could to encourage customers to buy name-brand ink and toner, claiming that aftermarket versions were ineffective or even caused damage to the machine. It was a sneaky ploy that might have worked, had it not been for the efforts of a retired grandmother living in a rural part of Washington state.

DeLores Williams had purchased a new HP printer for the purpose of printing photos of her fourteen grandkids. For the first year, the printer worked fine. Then suddenly, it started to go haywire. Williams had recently installed some off-brand ink cartridges she bought from Amazon, and after a month of light use the printer refused to work.

Williams knew there was nothing wrong with the ink she'd installed—she'd done her homework, and the third-party cartridges had great reviews. But there was no way to ignore or bypass the error messages she received when she went to print. When she called customer service, they told her she'd need to buy a new printer.

That was the wrong thing to say to this particular grandmother. As it turned out, Williams had worked in IT her entire career, so she immediately knew that something was amiss. Instead of giving HP more money, Williams launched a one-woman investigative journalism campaign and discovered that HP had not only tried to scare customers into buying exclusively its brand of ink—they'd even devoted considerable effort to surreptitiously delivering software updates that infected their own printer's hardware. The updates prevented cartridges without an HP chip from working in HP printers, effectively programming the machines to reject aftermarket brands. Her suspicions, in other words, had been correct: *it really was a scam.*

Unfortunately for HP, Williams was on a mission—and since she was now retired, she had plenty of time to spare. As a result of her efforts, HP ended up paying a class-action settlement for $1.5 million and issuing a new update that removed the previous restrictions.

If you've purchased knockoff-brand ink cartridges in the past few years, you can thank DeLores Williams for the savings. She took on Big Printer, and she won.

How can you beat a system that is rigged in favor of big corporations? Or even better—how can you profit from their evil acts?

In some cases, the answer is with data—the more, the better.

Beat the Bookies

Online sports bookkeepers ("bookies") employ hundreds of analysts. Their job is to make money for their employers at the expense of everyone else, and they're very good at it.

One of their responsibilities is to set the odds of betting markets. The goal is to do so in a way that is as attractive as possible to sports bettors (because if the odds of winning seem like too much of a long shot, customers will take their money elsewhere), while still maintaining enough edge for the bookmakers. For the bookies, an ideal "betting line" is similar to a casino game of roulette: players can sometimes come out ahead in the short term, but with repeated play over time, the house always wins.

Most people who bet seriously on sports develop systems for

beating the odds. Thanks to the power of Big Data, these systems can be quite sophisticated and are often based on a combination of mathematical modeling, research, and their own judgment. The problem is that the bookkeepers are doing this too, and they tend to be better at it.

In 2017, an international team of researchers led by a professor at the University of Tokyo decided to try something different: instead of attempting to outsmart the professionals with better predictions, they wanted to find a way to use the bookies' own predictions against them.

The team went into this experiment assuming that the predictions that online bookkeepers baked into their models were largely correct. But just to be safe, they decided to test this assumption by reviewing hundreds of thousands of records from past football games. The results showed that on aggregate, the bookkeepers' odds were usually spot-on.

Next, the team set out to identify what they called *mispriced odds,* or those instances when some bookkeepers offered odds that significantly differed from the consensus.

Mispriced odds can happen for a few different reasons. Most commonly, one bookie simply has too many bets placed on one team, so they offer slightly improved odds on the other team to attract more bettors and provide balance. Other times they want to poach bidders from competitors, so once again they offer more favorable terms.

The team's theory was: *If we bet on the games where the odds are mispriced, over time we'll win more than we lose.*

They set up a computer model to monitor betting odds in real time from more than thirty bookmakers for hundreds of games worldwide. After conducting more testing, they knew they were on to something. The practice trades they conducted consistently showed a higher return than random chance. Specifically, returns using the mispriced odds model averaged 3.5 percent, and returns from random chance betting averaged *negative* 3.3 percent.

Considering a hypothetical $50 bet on every game in their test model, the strategy returned an average profit of $98,865. The random chance model, on the other hand, returned an average loss of $93,563.*

If it sounds like $5,000 in profit wasn't much for all this effort, keep in mind that they were building a *model.* If, over time, you could consistently win with $50 bets, you could then raise your bets to earn a 3.5 percent return on $100, $200, or more.

Average sports betting strategy = -3.3 percent (negative)

"Mispriced odds" betting strategy = 3.5 percent (positive)

---

* The team noted: "The probability of obtaining a return greater than or equal to $98,865 in 56,435 bets using a random bet strategy is less than 1 in a billion" (https://arxiv.org/ftp/arxiv/papers/1710/1710.02824.pdf).

In looking at the historical data for sports betting, the team noticed that the odds tend to fluctuate a lot in the final few hours before closing. By applying their model to the last five hours before closing, it turned out, they were able to improve their odds and achieve a return of 5.5 percent, 2 percent higher than before.

So far, so good. The next step was to test their model using real money—which they did.

Next We Take Manchester

After opening accounts with dozens of online bookkeepers, the team began placing bets according to their model's recommendations.

Using $50 stakes for each bet, the team placed 265 bets over the next six months. By the end of the experiment, they'd achieved a profit of $957.50, equivalent to an 8.5 percent return on investment—an even better result than the practice rounds!

They'd done it: they'd beaten the system. Or at least, they'd *exploited* the system by finding the mispriced odds. Instead of trying to improve the predictions of hundreds of professional analysts, they'd taken those predictions at face value. Now they had a replicable strategy, along with an important advancement in research. Best of all, they had proved that the house doesn't necessarily always win after all.

The Price Is Right

The University of Tokyo researchers took on the bookies and won by capitalizing on mispriced odds. But it's possible to capitalize on discrepancies in pricing well beyond the world of sports betting: from buying up undervalued stocks, to holding out for price drops on airline tickets, to getting a great deal on everyday items like contact lenses.

I buy contact lenses whenever I'm out of the US, because the price is usually half of what I pay at home. No prescription or "doctor's authorization" is required. The same is true with certain medications. In many countries, many medications that require a prescription—and often a hefty copay—in the US are available over the counter, and cost much less.

Of course, highly addictive, harmful substances remain off-limits. But plenty of medications like antidepressants, treatments for sexual wellness, and even cancer drugs are available in some places. Buying these kinds of medications without a prescription is less risky than it sounds. A pharmacist is usually available to answer questions about dosage or side effects, not just to enforce the rules on what you can or can't have.

Travel is another example. The rules for airfare pricing are complex, but a simple one is that the price of international airfares is determined in large part by the country of origin. A ticket from New York to Bangkok, for example, will usually cost a lot more than Bangkok to New York. The effect is magnified even further with premium fares in First or Business Class. So if you live in the States but want to visit Asia two or more times a year, you can take advantage of this discrepancy by buying flights that begin from the cheaper country. Of course, you'll have to get to Bangkok (or wherever your actual destination is) the first time, but from there you're all set. For the second trip, and every one afterward, you just travel on round-trip flights *from* your destination instead of to it. Once you're back in New York with no future plans to visit Bangkok, you simply don't show up for the last segment of your itinerary.

Tired of Telemarketers? Sue Them

Who likes getting calls from telemarketers, offering you free iPads, car insurance, or home security systems? No one does—that is, no one except Andrew Perrong, a twenty-one-year-old from Huntingdon Valley, Pennsylvania, who has turned a recurring annoyance into a recurring source of income. He does this by happily accepting telemarketing calls and robocalls, listening to their sales pitch, then promptly suing the company behind the intrusion.

He's won settlements from Verizon and Citibank, in addition to many smaller companies, for violating provisions of the Telephone Consumer Protection Act, such as placing prerecorded calls without the recipient's consent, calling phone numbers on the Do Not Call list, and other sketchy practices. Most of these companies don't want the hassle or the negative publicity of court proceedings, so they pay up and Andrew goes away.

Andrew is tight-lipped about the results of his operation, citing "dozens" of in-process legal matters. But he's clearly rattled his opponents.

Dan Graham in Austin, Texas, has also turned to the legal system to take vengeance on telemarketers. At first, he wasn't trying to make money—he was just pissed off. On an average day he receives more than fifteen unwanted calls, and because of work and family commitments, it's not an option for him to simply ignore unknown numbers.

After one too many frustrating interruptions, he finally decided he'd had enough, and started filing complaints with the Better Business Bureau. From there, he moved on to filing actual lawsuits, typically in small claims court without an attorney. In less than a year, he collected more than $75,000.

PREMIUM SLEEP FOR FREE

It's hard to put a price on a good night's sleep. But what if you didn't have to?

There are dozens of mattress companies, but only a few mattress manufacturers. What does this mean? It means that most mattress brands are simply marketing companies. Their job is to convince you that their mattress is better, even if it's coming off the exact same assembly line as the other fancy brands.

Mattresses are a high-profit-margin business, so the companies that sell them can afford to be aggressive with marketing and discounts. Most of them have generous return policies, ranging from an industry standard of "100 nights" up to a full year. This is a big part of how they get away with charging exorbitant prices—people somehow feel less guilty about spending up to $25,000 (no kidding!) on a mattress when they know they can return it any time within those first three months, or even later.

Until I read a *New Yorker* article about the industry, I would have guessed that very few people bother to return their mattresses after so much time has passed—but I'd have been wrong. Industry return rates can be 15 percent or more, and the brands don't seem to care.

In fact, they even make it easy. If you request a return, the companies send someone out to pick up the mattress so you don't have to cart it outside or even attempt to squish it back into the bag it arrived in. Best of all, returned mattresses are typically donated to local shelters, so you can sleep easy knowing that your rejected mattress is going to someone who needs it, rather than to a landfill.

You might see where this is going: dozens of mattress companies, all offering a trial period of at least several months. So in theory, someone could keep "renting" new mattresses indefinitely.

In the name of research, I decided to try out the experiment. I ordered a new mattress from one of the big companies. A few days later, a heavy package showed up at my door. After setting up my new sleeping palace, I also set a reminder on my phone for ninety-eight days, two full days before running out the hundred-night guarantee.

I worried I'd grow so attached to it that I wouldn't want to send it back, but then I remembered: there's more where that came from. So as day ninety-eight approached, I picked out a new mattress from another company and ordered it to arrive on the same day I planned to send the original mattress back.

I'm now on mattress number three, another one with a hundred-night trial. If all goes as planned, by the time you read this, I should be on mattress number four or five. Sure, I'll probably have to put this experiment to bed eventually, but until then, I'm sleeping for free.

One note of caution if you decide to try this yourself: Be sure to carefully read the return policy before undertaking your own lifetime mattress trial experiment. You don't want to get stuck with an expensive mattress you didn't intend to keep.

How to Slay Goliath

Beating a system rigged against you isn't easy—just ask that team of researchers who tried to beat the bookies at their own game. Their research showed that it was mathematically possible to win, and they came up with a clever strategy that proved it. Unfortunately, that's not the end of the story.

After their initial victory, it wasn't long before the researchers ran into roadblocks. Now, when the team went to place bets on games their model recommended, they encountered system limitations. This happened over and over, most frequently in the form of betting limits. They could put as much money as they wanted on certain bets, but on games with positive expected value they were allowed to bet only $10 to $20, and sometimes as little as $1. Other times they couldn't place a bet at all, and instead encountered an error message claiming that some sort of "manual inspection" was required. Clearly the bookies were onto them.

The researchers tried to get around these roadblocks by opening new accounts. But it turned out that the bookies kept a list of IP addresses connected with "problem customers" (i.e., those who committed the cardinal sin of winning). And as soon as someone signed up for a new account with a known IP address, the account would get flagged and limited. It turned out that not only were the bookmakers highly skilled at predicting the outcomes of games, they were also very good at *preventing bettors from winning*.

The situation seemed comparable to what happens if you try to count cards in Las Vegas. It's perfectly legal to count cards in a game of blackjack, and if you do it properly, you can win big. But that's easier said than done, as the casinos are really good at getting in your way. When casino staff identify the small minority of players who manage to win consistently, the pit bosses simply ban them from playing. So yeah, counting cards in Vegas is totally cool, but counting cards and *winning* is unacceptable.

Eventually, the research team chose to call it a day and return to their real jobs as nongambling professors. In the last sentence of their report, they wrote, "Because bookmakers' restrictions turned the betting experience increasingly difficult, we decided to end our betting experiment."

The report left no doubt: Goliath would not go down without a fight.

RENTING A CAR FROM HERTZ CAN PUT YOU IN JAIL

A lifelong expert on travel and loyalty programs, Gary Leff normally writes about airfare deals and packing tips.

Several years ago, though, he began chronicling something strange: the number of Hertz customers who ended up being detained, arrested, and sometimes held in jail *for weeks,* all due to cases of mistaken identity.

It gets worse: Hertz customers keep getting thrown in jail because the company keeps falsely accusing them of stealing its vehicles.

I read Gary's blog daily, and at first I didn't think much about these bizarre incidents. But pretty soon it became a bizarre *pattern* that was too hard to ignore.

It's no exaggeration to say that Hertz is responsible for *hundreds* of false arrests. One customer, James Tolen, was arrested for driving a car Hertz had reported stolen three months earlier—*before* renting it to him! Another customer was jailed for six months after Hertz reported his rental car stolen. In reality, he had returned it and paid the bill in full. Others have been arrested at gunpoint in front of their young children, even when they had the rental paperwork in the car.

Perhaps most egregious of all, a customer was arrested four separate times and held for more than thirty days in jail, *where she suffered a miscarriage*.

How in the world does this keep happening? Believe it or not, the executives at Hertz don't have a good answer, or even any real answer at all. The best they've come up with is "Yeah, this is an industry-wide problem"—except it's happening only with their customers, so, no.*

---

* Again, I'm not making this up! It sounds incredible but it's well documented. Also, the customer who had a miscarriage while falsely imprisoned *was a Hertz Platinum member.*

Finally, toward the end of 2022, the company agreed to pay $168 million to settle 364 claims related to these false arrests. Other litigants (yes, there are more!) who opted out of the class-action suit are continuing with their claims.

Lesson: If you rent a car from Hertz, be prepared to go to jail. Though you might, eventually, be able to profit from it.

Fighting back against a system rigged in favor of big corporations and against ordinary creators is what the Money Revolution is all about. Don't want to get arrested for driving a rental car you paid for? Try using a peer-to-peer service instead of a company that owns and controls its own fleet. Fed up with how sports bookies rig the odds in their favor? Learn to use the blockchain betting sites mentioned in chapter three.

As for McDonald's, it can't seem to stay out of trouble. As I was finishing this book, the company continued its legal battle with Jeremy O'Sullivan and Melissa Nelson, the owners of the service that helped put the power of soft serve back into the hands of McDonald's franchisees. O'Sullivan and Nelson have filed suit, alleging that McDonald's and Taylor Company (the McDonald's vendor that services the machines) colluded to keep a much better product off the market. They're seeking a jury trial and "no less" than $900 million in damages.

Chapter Ten

Don't Inform, Transform

CONCEPT: Online education has shifted. Merely providing information and expecting students to learn on their own is no longer sufficient. Instead, the most successful educators are the ones focused on creating transformative experiences.

Woniya Thibeault spends her days sewing clothes from animal hides. She's a leader in the "primitive skills movement," which values complete self-sufficiency in wilderness settings.

For more than twenty years she'd made her living as a teacher of "ancestral skills," in homesteads in rural Oregon and Wisconsin. For much of that time, her programs served a small community of outdoorsy folks. These days, however, most of her students are urban professionals who want to immerse themselves in wilderness living, learning skills like hide tanning, flint sharpening, and deciphering bird language.

Two things changed her small following to a very large one: a reality-TV show, and the global pandemic.

On the TV series *Alone*, contestants are dropped off at wilderness points, where they must survive in the elements for months at a time. At any point they can "tap out" to be rescued by a helicopter, but whoever endures until the end wins a large cash prize. (This being a reality show, contestants are also given several cameras, along with the direction to record their attempts at foraging for berries and eluding grizzly bears.)

Thibeault joined the cast of contestants for season six, and ended her stint in the Arctic Circle after seventy-three days. She then returned for a special "all-star" season, during which she became the first woman ever to win, while also setting a show record for the most cumulative days alone in the wilderness.

The first season that featured Thibeault aired in 2020, just as the pandemic was in full force. More than three million people with extra time on their hands watched the show that year, bringing Thibeault new attention.

She now offers a range of online experiences for her growing fan base, including a Patreon membership and several on-demand courses. The flagship experience, however, is a cohort-based course she runs twice a year. It's called the Buckskin Revolution Academy, which is more or less exactly what it sounds like.

Enrollment in the flagship course costs $287 and now sells out quickly each time it opens. Want to know how to safely eat roadkill? She's got you covered. Need to start a fire without matches? That's in week two.

In another course, priced at only $92, students can learn the fundamentals of buckskin sewing. Those who wish to take these skills to the next level can sign up for a course on how to transform raw deer hides into "Brain Tanned Buckskin." During this three-day experience, "everyone will participate hands-on in every stage of tanning, including hide prep, scraping, dressing, softening, and smoking," according to the course description.

The Buckskin Revolution grew by leaps and bounds during the pandemic, for a few reasons. Not only were people getting more comfortable with meeting remotely, all of a sudden the desire to learn survival skills seemed more urgent. And with so many people trapped in their homes, the longing to connect with nature, whether as a skill, a hobby, or an apocalypse backup plan, exploded.

As her fame and following continued to grow, Thibeault branched out into an entirely different kind of survival skills education, including consulting services for aspiring *Alone* contestants, as well as consulting for authors, producers, and filmmakers "working to create a book, television show, movie or something similar that involves aspects of wilderness survival, ancestral skills, homesteading or off-grid living."

Massive Online Courses That No One Finishes

In 2008, higher education got life-hacked. Or at least, that's how it seemed to anyone who read the breathless features in mainstream news outlets describing the popularity of a new innovation: massive open online courses. Known as MOOCs, these courses were free, open to anyone, and taught by professors from some of the most prestigious universities in the world. And because they were virtual and unconstrained by the spatial limitations of a physical classroom, a course could attract tens of thousands of eager enrollees—and many did.

In a few cases, *hundreds of thousands* of students signed up *for a single course.* One Chinese professor who taught more than 50,000 students a quarter was so enthralled by this new model, he ended up quitting his day job to run the course full-time.

The MOOC model was pioneered at the University of Manitoba in 2008, and soon grew to include offerings from Harvard, Stanford, MIT, and many other elite institutions worldwide. In some cases, the courses were even billed as equivalent to a university's flagship education—the same courses that require highly competitive applications for the in-person experience. Only, these versions were available to anyone who took ten minutes out of their day to sign up.

You know the saying "Knowledge is power." Well, power was

now democratized! Anyone could now get a Harvard education on demand, for free. Surely all those old-school universities would soon go bankrupt. Peace on earth was close at hand.

MOOCs were supposed to upend the world of higher education—and for a brief period, they sort of did. But in the long run, they turned out to be far less revolutionary than predicted.

The institutions that allowed their content to be streamed for free had been worried that MOOCs would devalue the in-person experience—you know, that experience they sold for $40,000 or more each year to young, traditional students attending on campus. But it turned out they were worried about the wrong thing.

The fact that anyone could take every MIT class online for free didn't result in fewer people wanting to attend MIT. If anything, the free classes acted as a lead-generation tool that got *more* people interested in applying. So what happened? In short, the hype soon fizzled. MOOCs were groundbreaking in theory, but in practice they also revealed a glaring problem.

These were the best courses, taught by the most engaging professors, at highly selective institutions. You could take them for free. You could watch them on a tablet or smartphone. It was incredibly easy!

But as easy as it was to attend a course, it was even easier to enroll and then never show up. The great majority of students, sometimes more than 95 percent, never returned after watching a couple of introductory lectures, and in some cases, only a quarter of the people who purchased an on-demand course *even logged in.* Studies consistently put the average MOOC completion rate in the 5 to 15 percent range. Just consider how low that is: *as many as nineteen out of twenty students dropped out.*

By comparison, something like 60 percent of students who enroll in college will complete their degrees. Even among community colleges, which typically serve students simultaneously juggling full-time jobs and child care, the graduation rate is somewhere around 40 percent.

Clearly, something went wrong.

Was It Just Because They Were Free? (Nope.)

At the time, many attributed the dismal completion rate to the fact that MOOCs are typically free, so anyone can sign up on a whim without any incentive to see things through. This theory makes intuitive sense: when I first discovered Coursera, which offers a large number of introductory courses from highly rated university professors, I loved the idea. I signed up for a world history course that I dutifully watched all the way through.

Then I signed up for one on constitutional law, and another one on coding Python. I didn't make it past the second video for either one. Why should I? If I got bored, there were plenty of others to choose from.

You'd think having skin in the game might make a difference. Maybe if I'd had to pay something for my constitutional law or

Python courses, I wouldn't have abandoned them so quickly. Then again, I once bought a marketing course that cost more than $1,000, and I never watched any of it. And I'm far from the only one.

It turns out that putting a price tag on courses doesn't boost completion rates in the way you might expect. Even when they pay good money, many people who register for online courses still don't actually see them through. In fact, this is not the exception; it's the rule.

On the surface, it seems weird: Why in the world would people spend money on educational products they never use? But it's no weirder than paying $100 a month for a gym membership you end up using only once or twice a year.

As someone who's taught and sold lots of courses, I've also been on the other side of this equation. In my early days as a course creator, sometimes I'd go to help with a password reset request, only to discover that the buyer had never set a password in the first place. This seemed unusual, especially in cases where more than a year had passed since they made the purchase.

The problem is that the very benefit of on-demand education ("Buy it now and access it anytime!") is also a barrier to consuming the content and doing the work. Because you can access on-demand information whenever you want, you tend to put it off until later—especially in the case of self-paced learning, where there's no one looking over your shoulder or tracking your progress.

Good intentions aren't enough to achieve lasting change. And given the choice between watching educational course videos and the latest bingeable TV series, maybe it's only natural that people tend to defer the course experience over and over.

Transformation, Not Information

Even though the benefits of MOOCs weren't as life-changing as promised, it's fair to say that they "democratized information," at least to a certain extent. The problem is that to truly learn something, mere information is rarely enough.

Imagine you have a goal of finally learning to speak Spanish. You buy an expensive language-learning program, committing to make an investment in yourself. Then you get off track somehow. Maybe you get busy, or bored, or maybe it just dawns on you that you're not going to master the language as quickly as you thought. Now you feel worse than you did before starting, but you don't ask for a refund, because you assume it's your fault.

If you're selling language-learning programs, you could simply accept that this is how it goes for many buyers. Or you could ask: What would happen if you did everything you could to improve the learning experience, so more buyers would *want* to stick around?

You could start with a *strong onboarding plan*, making sure that students get set up quickly and immediately jump into lesson one. You could add in *elements of gamification,* where they earn badges for completing lessons in a certain amount of time. You could set up a process for *outreach and follow-up,* where you or an assistant checks in with them regularly to see how they're doing. None of these solutions solves every problem, but they all help.

In the end, you wouldn't have just handed over a bunch of information, you would have helped someone achieve an important goal.

In other words, you'd have created much more value, and in turn, your students would become your ambassadors. "Your Spanish is amazing!" their friends would say.

"*¡Gracias!*" they'd reply. "This amazing program I bought has really helped me... I'll send you the link."

This is the shift that online education is heading toward: *transformation above information.* Creators who understand this principle are positioned to succeed.

Online Education: From the Stone Age to Today

The world of individual course creation has gone through a series of stages not unlike the archaeological stages of prehistoric human civilization. We can label them as follows: the Stone Age, the Bronze Age, the Iron Age, and now the Modern Age.

Stone Age — good for early adopters

The early days of online education were a good time to be a creator. Some products sold insanely well. Joel Runyon, a friend of mine, earned a six-figure income for several years entirely through the sale of an ebook on getting "impossible" abs. That was it — once he'd written and published it, he did nothing for it aside from collecting payments and occasionally answering support questions.

Another friend sold ebooks on how to write ebooks, the ultimate meta move, and also pulled in a ton of money. Today, as you might have guessed, making money from "e-products" isn't what it used to be. After all, for those who want to get ripped, the same info is freely available in a few short YouTube videos. Joel's abs book was the right product at the right time, but time and technology eventually marched on.

Bronze Age — good for platforms, sort of good for creators

During the Bronze Age, human societies across Europe, ancient Egypt, and Asia developed one of the first known industrial processes for the production of metals, spawning several regional marketplaces in which bronze items could be traded. Similarly, in the Bronze Age of online education, multiple platforms including

Udacity, Skillshare, Coursera, and CreativeLive emerged. They functioned as marketplaces where lots of individual creators could put their talents up for sale. The platforms would market and host the courses, paying the creator a share of the revenue and keeping a much larger share for themselves.*

But the platforms benefited more than the individual creators. If anything, the goals of creators and platforms were at odds. The platforms, typically funded by venture capital, wanted more than anything to grow their user base. Creators were essentially subcontractors who enabled this growth. The more creators they hosted, the more users they would attract, the platforms reasoned. And they may have been right, at least at first. But the ones who bore the brunt of this strategy were the creators themselves. If you offer a class on T-shirt quilting or drum tuning, and the platform that hosts it keeps on adding more and more courses on the same topic, your share of the profit will eventually be diluted.

Of course, creators didn't love the transactional nature of this relationship (*or* the imbalanced profit share), but they also didn't have a ton of other options. The platforms made some things easy and allowed them to reach more students, at least potentially. A few of them ended up doing very well. Many others did *just okay.*

---

* In some cases, creators earn as little as 5 percent of the profits from marketplace platforms.

Iron Age — better for creators, but still not perfect

Recognizing the imbalance, a new wave of start-ups committed to serve creators, giving them (well, *selling* them) the toolkit they needed to own more of the course creation process, as well as more of the profits—just like in the original Iron Age, when metal production advanced to the point where an array of advanced tools could be made available to the masses.

These companies—Thinkific, Teachable, ConvertKit, to name a few—scaled their pricing depending on usage, so that successful creators would pay higher fees but would presumably be earning more than enough income to offset the cost. In short, the creators had more control.

So far, so good...but something was missing.

What's Missing? Students!

There was one more problem that none of these models addressed directly: None of them was focused squarely on what online learners actually wanted.

I used to think that the "convenience" of online courses was the thing people were willing to pay for, but I'm not sure that assumption has held up. Sure, convenience has value, but it falls short of being a competitive advantage. In the same way that Amazon has turned fast, free shipping into the norm—"What do you mean it will take a week to arrive?!"—the ability to consume content wherever and whenever you want to has become an expected standard.

We're now in a fourth phase of educational content creation where the winners are the ones who deliver something much more valuable than convenient, easy access to information. They are the ones who put in the effort to create *transformational experiences* for their students.

What matters now in online education is *impact*. It's not just about delivering accurate information; it's about making certain that the relevant information can be absorbed and applied.

The days of selling hundreds of thousands of dollars in ebooks on six-pack abs are over, at least for most people. But the e-learning market is far from dead: by one estimate, it will soon reach $325 billion a year.

Today's most successful course creators believe that the cohort-based course model (CBC) combines the advantages of the marketplace and toolkit models with an experiential approach that's geared toward helping students achieve their desired results.

Let's look at a creator who saw this change coming and got in on the ground floor.

Building a Second Brain

Tiago Forte could have been a diplomat, and he nearly was. Growing up in a half-Brazilian, half-Filipino household in Orange County, he learned multiple languages and studied a range of subjects. After graduating from college, he served in the Peace Corps for two years, then went to work as a junior analyst for a French start-up.

Through it all he kept coming back to the same theme: a love of knowledge, but a sense of overwhelm in managing it all. Tiago loved learning and was frustrated with how little knowledge he typically retained. "We feel this pressure to constantly be improving ourselves," he wrote in a blog post, "but so much of what we consume just goes in one ear and out the other." He then set out to build a system that would help him keep up with all the information he absorbed.

As this was happening, Tiago was dealing with a mysterious illness that had suddenly appeared. He visited doctor after doctor in a series of endless referrals, but none managed to come up with a diagnosis, let alone a cure.

At some point he started doing his own research. He talked with specialists, read medical journals, and did countless diagnostic tests. There was no central file for all the medical consultations he'd had, so he made one by scanning his patient records along with years' worth of his own notes and observations, and tagged all the content so it would be easier to retrieve a piece of information whenever it was needed. This experience led him to think more seriously about the field of personal knowledge management, and soon he had created a system for dealing with staggering amounts of information.

After some encouragement from his colleagues, he decided to create a course on the method. What was originally just a proof of concept soon turned into something much bigger: a wildly expansive cohort-based course called Building a Second Brain.

The course was built with a focus on real-time interactions with students, as opposed to prerecorded material. "With the live teaching model, there's nowhere to hide," Tiago told me. He also assigned students to small groups where they could check in with one another, even in the middle of a teaching session. In start-up terms: accountability became a competitive advantage.

As he ran additional cohorts, more and more people signed up. Then, as most people were stuck indoors for large parts of 2020, the business exploded. In one cohort he had more than 1,000 paying students.

Tuition starts at $1,500, with the option to pay more for higher tiers that offer more personalized support. Financially, this adds up to millions of dollars—all from an online course that Tiago offers just two or three times a year.

BETTER CAT VIDEOS IN 30 DAYS

Are your cat videos suffering from blurred images or uncooperative subjects? The new Better Cat Videos in 30 Days course will help!

The course consists of:

- 12 on-demand video modules (watch meow or later)
- 5 weekly "ask me anything" Zoom meetings
- 60-day post-course check-in
- A private community to share tips, stories, and catnip recipes

By the end of the course, you'll have gained an incredible amount of knowledge and start feline more confident in your videography skills.

Price: $10,000

Sign up now and get ready to go viral!

Want to Teach a Cohort-Based Course? Become a Maven

Maven (maven.com) is both an accelerator program for aspiring course creators and a platform that offers numerous cohort-based courses for users. When you get trained through Maven, you gain the ability to market your courses directly to its large community of users. (Maven, of course, takes a cut of your earnings.)

The platform is tech- and start-up–heavy, but other options such as language learning or growing a personal brand are also featured. A few examples:

- Financial Statements Explained Simply
- User Research Bootcamp
- Measuring Development Team Performance
- Become a Web3 Leader
- Impactful Social Writing

These are all cohort-based courses, meaning that users register for a specific start and end date, then meet online regularly to go through the course together. That's the main difference between a program like Maven's and those of many other "course creator" tools: most of the others aren't focused on the unique aspects of the cohort-based model.

How to Transform Lives

At this point you might be thinking, *Great, all I need to do is figure out how to transform people's lives, and then I'll be all set!* Well, perhaps it sounds intimidating when you put it that way, but in reality it's not so difficult. The characteristics of transformative learning are far from elusive. We can identify them right here.

1. **Work from a "student first" mindset.** Just think, *What's best for students?* at every step in the process. When picking a topic, don't ask *What I am most interested in teaching?* Instead, ask *What do other people want to learn?*

   The best topics have a clearly defined benefit. Topics that can be applied in the workplace are always good, especially since course participants can sometimes get reimbursed by their employers.

   The benefit your course delivers will also impact the price you're able to charge. You can probably charge more for an online course that helps hedge fund traders be more effective at picking tech stocks, for example, than one that teaches aspiring crafters how to knit socks.

   Remember Miss Excel, the social media sensation who's earning millions from courses on using spreadsheets: her courses provide a clear benefit (more productivity, less frustration) that makes it easy to charge a premium.

2. **Focus on *outcomes*.** Once you know what you want to teach, your next step is to break up the material into a series of modular lessons.

   Most lessons consist of a primary means of delivering the material (typically video lectures) along with some supplemental materials that can be delivered in any number of formats.

One way to keep the emphasis on results is to have a concrete objective (or "learning outcome") for each lesson, video, class discussion, or other course component. It's often worded like this:

After watching this short video, students will be able to [do something specific].

Keep learning outcomes short and incremental. If your course is about personal finance, a learning outcome for one module might be "Students will learn how to direct-deposit a portion of their paycheck into a retirement savings account."

You *wouldn't* want an outcome for a single module such as "Students will learn how to make and keep a budget." There are a lot of steps to a process like that, and when you stick to a single goal per video (or module, lesson, discussion, etc.), students will feel a sense of accomplishment after each one they finish.

3. **Don't pack too much in.** If you want to make a successful cohort-based course, you need to transfer a skill or set of knowledge from your head to your students. But notice that I said *a* skill or set of knowledge—not dozens of skills or sets of knowledge. Resist the urge to teach them

everything you know about a topic. Unless they've purchased a course on home remodeling, they don't want the kitchen sink!

You may be tempted to "go above and beyond" or show off all the advanced things you know, but it's much better to give people the basics they need. The goal here is quality of learning, not quantity. At the same time, don't assume that your students come with any preexisting knowledge of the topic beyond what the average person would have. Just because something is obvious to you, that doesn't mean it's obvious to your students—that's why you're teaching the course and they're taking it.

Remember, it's not about you, it's about them! Your results will ultimately hinge on your ability to deliver results for them.

4. **Be present.** It's not enough to simply show up to teach the course; you should also make yourself available to answer questions, publish updates, and generally be present so that student motivation remains high.

When I took Tiago's Building a Second Brain course, I was surprised by how many people showed up to weekly lectures—especially since some of them were alumni who'd been through the material before.

That's when I realized that students weren't *just* showing up to learn (or relearn) the specific techniques. They were also coming for the sense of community and connection Tiago created—something that can't be faked.

The community aspect of cohort-based courses is critical. So in addition to being present for your students, consider offering regular online meet-ups where participants can ask questions and be present with one another.

5. **Focus on storytelling.** This principle applies to the videos you record for the course, as well as the ones you make for marketing. Posting a couple of times on social media and waiting for sign-ups to flood in is not an effective marketing strategy. Be passionate and clearly explain what problem your course will solve, and why someone should take action and sign up.

   For the course itself, develop a narrative arc that takes your students on a journey from problem to solution. In her Buckskin Academy, Woniya Thibeault tells a story of self-sufficiency and connection with the natural world throughout the course. The goal is for students to remember what inspired them to sign up for the course in the first place as they progress through each module.

A SHORT COURSE IN CREATING COURSE DELIVERABLES

Once you have your topic and have decided how you'll deliver it, you need to get to work.

Depending on what you'll be teaching, this process can take anywhere from a week to several months. But the more you can break it down into a series of checklists, the easier it will be.

For example, if you're making a series of videos, you'll need to:

- Make a list of each video.
- Create a learning outcome for each video (what will students know how to do after watching it?).
- Write a script for each video (don't try to "wing it").
- Decide how you'll film each video.
- Rehearse, film, and edit each video.
- Add videos to the course interface where students can access them.
- Publish a schedule of when each video will be released.
- Plan for any live sessions, including scripts or at least a detailed outline for whatever you plan to teach.

It's Good That It's Hard (Otherwise, Everyone Would Do It)

The barriers to making money through online education have never been lower. But at the same time, the bar of *quality* has been raised—and this is a good thing! Sure, it takes a lot more work to design a totally immersive course, but when you do, *students actually learn.*

As an online educator seeking to get paid from courses you create, you have a couple of options: a) provide a mediocre experience and hope no one notices, or b) study what makes for a *great* online learning experience, and give it your own creative spin.

Choose option b, and you can charge higher prices, confident that it's not marketing hype that's selling your experience, but the transformation you provide. The more thought you put into the design of your course, the harder it will be to copy, because it's unique to you.

Do this well, and you'll have constructed a moat—to use another start-up term—that serves as a barrier against competition. Building a moat can be time-intensive. But once you've built it, you're protected from competitors and poised to thrive.

Chapter Eleven

To End Capitalism, Buy This Book

CONCEPT: Surveys show that capitalism is about as popular as a root canal for most Gen Zers, who reject the traditional exchange of labor for wages. The "antiwork" movement seeks to rebalance power between employers and employees, and others are trying to jumpstart the barter economy. Meanwhile, an army of amateur day traders takes a different approach to the redistribution of wealth and power.

In the summer of 2020, a Black woman named Moirha Smith started a Google Doc where other Black people could sign up to receive voluntary payments from white people: an experiment in "DIY Reparations," as an NPR episode later called it.

This was the summer when Black Lives Matter protests were taking place everywhere. In Smith's home state of Vermont—the whitest in the country—most of the protestors were white, and Smith felt that some were on the streets less because they were committed to systematic change, but because "it was the cool thing to do." So together with a few friends, she decided to issue a challenge to white people, inviting them to put their money where their mouths were and donate directly to Black Vermonters.

Over the next sixty days, tens of thousands of dollars of "wealth transfers" took place, as did many difficult but important household conversations about what white Americans owe the descendants of former slaves.

Of course, redistributing wealth via a Google Doc is probably not the most effective (or most scalable) way to redress hundreds of years of racial injustice. Besides, reparations are supposed to come from the government, right?

Well, it wasn't perfect, but it was a bold effort that got a lot of people thinking. Plus, reparations from the government aren't exactly forthcoming anytime soon, and this movement brought in a lot of money in a short period of time.

In the era of Gonzo Capitalism, crowdfunding has been reconfigured to the point where the right campaign can take on a life of its own, attracting hundreds of thousands of dollars from hordes of backers and cheerleaders. In the past, a successful campaign required weeks of careful planning, along with a parade of PR pitches in search of media coverage. Some still benefit from such efforts, but for others, all they need is the right viral moment.

Here's a very different example: Brian Kolfage, an air force veteran and Trump supporter, started his own "Build a Wall" fundraiser in an attempt to help finance the former president's quixotic obsession. Kolfage brought in far, far more than he anticipated—$25 million, to be precise—but he ended up being indicted along with Steve Bannon for defrauding his campaign's backers.

These goals ("Transfer generational wealth" and "Build Trump's border wall") are ideological near opposites, yet they had one thing in common: each tapped into powerful, even fervent, beliefs among the groups where they found support. They then drew upon these heightened emotions to quickly raise large sums of money.

Let's Talk About Capitalism

As I was working on this book, I kept noticing how shifts in technology accompanied shifts in attitudes toward the prevailing economic order. (It wasn't always clear which came first.)

The pandemic led to the largest reorganization of employment in world history. Entire industries were rendered obsolete, some temporarily and some permanently, and millions of workers were sent home. Stimulus packages of billions of dollars were deployed by governments worldwide. Money rained from the sky!

With a deadly, mysterious virus on the loose — and at least one unexpected bonus check in their bank accounts — many people used the experience to reinvent themselves and find a sense of purpose. In the wake of Black Lives Matter protests, campaigns like Vermont's "DIY Reparations" took on outsized importance.

Meanwhile, labor unions were becoming cool again, with unionization efforts at companies like Amazon and Starbucks spurring a nationwide surge in labor organizing.

The common goal uniting all these movements was clear: the redistribution of wealth to groups that had been systematically exploited. Or as some of the groups saw it: power was flowing back into the hands of the people, and they were determined to use it.

To Work or Not to Work

The movement known as antiwork has millions of followers on Reddit. As the name suggests, it exists "to end work," as we know it — or at least to support conversations around that topic. Posts regularly feature horror stories of bosses making egregious demands of employees, especially low-wage employees, and comment threads are dominated by tips and support for workers, typically encouraging them to do as little as possible without getting fired. (Or, sometimes, to get fired and then file lawsuits.)

A related community, Malicious Compliance, is full of stories from workers who accommodated their employers' demands to the letter, but did so in ways that were designed to backfire on the employer. Does your boss insist you clock out at 5:00 p.m., and not a minute earlier? Okay, but if your workday ends at 5:00 on the dot, refuse to serve the important customer who walks in at 5:02. If a micromanaging manager tells you to stop helping out other departments, follow his orders until *his* boss asks for your help, then gets upset when you say you've been forbidden to do so by your manager.

On the surface, these communities might seem to represent the polar opposite of the overemployed movement, chronicled in chapter three. The people working two or more full-time jobs on the sly have to work hard to keep up appearances, while those generally opposed to the employer-employee model deliberately do the bare minimum.

But I see them as more aligned than opposed. Both are subversive methods of redistributing power and capital from employers to employees. One of them—the overemployed approach—is just a lot more lucrative.

Taken all together, it's clear that many people think much differently about capitalism now than they did just a couple of decades ago. In fact, as a recent study revealed, socialism is now as popular as capitalism among Gen Z.

It's, Like, the System Is the Problem

I should admit my own bias here: I'm a capitalist! Or at least, I always assumed I was, which is why I've found some of the recent anticapitalism rhetoric interesting.

Before writing this chapter, I surveyed some of my readers to ask for their views on capitalism. What I found confirmed the research: they aren't big fans.

Since several of my books are about making money, I wondered what exactly made them attractive to so many fervent anti-capitalists. Making it even more confusing, some of the readers who responded were also frequent listeners to my daily podcast, *Side Hustle School*. The entire purpose of the show is to highlight stories of people earning extra income apart from their day job—capitalism is the point!

How could someone be a fan of a podcast about making money while also holding a negative view of an economic system that revolved around making money? One answer, I realized, was that their definition of modern capitalism could be very different from that of older generations.

So in addition to asking for my readers' views on the topic, I also asked a simpler question: "What is capitalism?"

I received a flood of replies to that question as well. Some offered a straightforward dictionary definition, but many of the others *clearly had feelings* on this topic. A brief selection:

> *Wealth inequality and the exploitation of labor*
> *Pursuit of profits above all else*
> *Banks controlling who can have money and who cannot*
> *A system that oppresses poor people*
> *A scam for the rich to get richer*
> *A broken system that treats humans like machines*

The list went on and on. To be clear, these were the negative responses—I also received positive ones, like "Capitalism is the economic system that allows me to start and run my own business." But since I'd always thought more along those lines myself, I was interested in opinions that were different than mine.

Many readers made a distinction between a dictionary definition of capitalism (an "economic system") and what they termed *late-stage capitalism*: a more nefarious version of capitalism associated with the concentration of wealth among the 1 percent, the patriarchy, and racism.

According to Google Trends, the use of this phrase has tripled in recent years. Blaming late-stage capitalism for the mundane problems of life has also become a bit of a meme. Spill your coffee? *Thanks, late-stage capitalism.* Stuck in a middle seat on your flight? *Late-stage capitalism strikes again!*

A few years back, Kendall Jenner starred in a Pepsi ad that caused quite a bit of controversy. It opens with shots of protestors marching in the streets, then cuts to several uniformed police officers standing by to intervene. Jenner saunters over and hands a cop a Pepsi—and suddenly, the potential clash between activists and police is avoided, and all is right with the world.

Almost immediately, the ad was widely criticized for attempting to commercialize civic action while making light of the Black Lives Matters movement and the problem of police brutality. The idea that a billionaire (Kendall Jenner) and a massive corporation (Pepsi) could bring people together, as the ad suggested, was offensive, and the ad was eventually pulled. But the outrage it inspired tells us a lot about what people hate about modern capitalism—the fact that the rich *do* just keep getting richer, all while trivializing everyone else's problems.

Putting all this together, I began to formulate a theory. The theory is: Being an anticapitalist and wanting to make money aren't conflicting ideologies after all. Because if the game is already rigged against you, you might as well learn to find an edge and get what you can for yourself.

It's an odd mash-up, just like so many other things in the age of Gonzo Capitalism. If you think about it *too* much, it makes your head hurt. But if you consider the contradictions in their proper context, things start to make sense.

"DO THESE ADS SUCK?" . . .

"NO, GIVE US MORE!"

Despite not being averse to the model of capitalism, I'd always shied away from endorsing brands or otherwise working with big corporations. I prided myself on being fully independent, and I assumed that many of my readers expected me to stay that way.

That's why I was initially reluctant to enter the podcast world, which is driven in large part by advertising. The model is well established: content is free for listeners, but supported by advertisers. I worried, though, that my readers would think I'd sold out. I imagined being deluged with complaints from disappointed fans.

To my surprise, not only did no one complain when I jumped into podcasting, some readers actually seemed to appreciate the model. Toward the end of the show's first season, I went on a book tour. At one event, a woman stood up, totally unprompted, to say thanks for introducing her to the product made by one of my sponsors. I was shocked.

But now that I've hosted the show for five years and counting, it makes sense: as long as you don't compromise too much, and the ads don't get too annoying, it seems that most people are happy to listen to a few ads when they are getting something for free.

A New Idea That Will Change ~~Everything~~ Very Little

Another example of a movement seeking to unwind capitalism (or at least remix it) is through something known as a DAO.

What's a DAO? It's a *decentralized autonomous organization*, also known as an organization governed entirely by its members, rather than by executives or some secretive leadership body.

DAOs are usually organized around a specific project or goal. If you issue a cryptocurrency token, for example, you might set up a DAO to raise funds, manage transaction records, and facilitate transfers.

Sometimes, leaders are elected by members of the DAO, and in other cases there are no formal leadership roles at all. Anyone can put forth a proposal for the whole group to vote on, and the majority sets the rules.

Participating in a DAO means being part of governance. In practical terms, this means you contribute to conversations and play a role in decision-making. The utopian view of DAOs is "Everyone has a voice!"

A more skeptical view is that it's hard to reach consensus decisions with thousands of people, so inevitably some set of de facto leaders will emerge and end up steering the ship. Plus while everyone might have a voice, not everyone has an *equal* voice: the more shares or tokens you own in a decentralized protocol, the more voting power you typically have. And protests, revolts, and power grabs happen all the time—just as they do at other kinds of organizations.

DAOs also rely on complex technology, like blockchain ledgers and distributed databases, in order to function properly. With membership being largely anonymous, plus the fact that most investors don't understand the underlying technology, all but the most ardent proponents of decentralized financial products are understandably wary of participating . As a result, many attempts to raise large sums of money—like one by a group of football fans who put together a DAO to facilitate the purchase of the Denver Broncos—haven't worked. In one particularly famous example, a DAO that was set up to buy a rare first printing of the US Constitution on auction at Sotheby's managed to raise $47 million from 17,000 contributors in less than seventy-two hours, but still lost to a hedge fund founder in a bidding war.

So if the loudest voices are the ones that get heard, and the highest-status members get to have the most influence over the decision-making, is it really that different from any other type of entity?

HOW TO RIG A (DAO) ELECTION

With voting power determined by how many shares or tokens you own, one could argue that DAO elections are already set up to favor the rich.

But even if you have a very small ownership stake in a DAO, there are some tried-and-true tactics you can deploy to make your vote count.

- **Create a coalition, and get your votes in early.** Momentum often carries the day, so line up blocks of supporters to vote as early as possible. The tally of results is shown in real time, so anyone who arrives on the voting website will see that you're winning by a lot.
- **Set up a vote with no good options.** Should our organization hack the treasury and run off with the money, or just hack the treasury and keep the money for ourselves? Hey, it's democracy—you can decide!
- **Split the vote by creating two versions of the least-desired option.** I saw this done in a vote over how to discipline a founder who'd made a big mistake that cost the community a lot of money. The options were:
  - A) Remove the founder from the executive team entirely.
  - B) Keep the founder on the executive team, but remove him from his role as CEO.
  - C) Do nothing.

In this case, the votes for A and B ended up being split, meaning that option C—to do nothing at all—carried the day. It goes to show that rule "by the people" works as well in a decentralized organization as it does in the real world, which is to say: sometimes not at all.

A Short Guide to Stock Price Fixing

Of course, not all anticapitalists hate capitalism—or at least not the part that involves the stock market. In fact, some embrace it to a manic degree.

By now, you've heard the story of GameStop, when an eight-million-strong army on Reddit came together to support a failing chain of video game stores. Their goal was to profit from an imbalance of short positions held by hedge funds, but they were just as motivated by the idea of "the common man" with a day-trading account taking down the establishment players who were betting big money that the company's share price had nowhere to go but down.

It's illegal for you and me to collude in buying shares to drive up the price of a stock. Those pesky laws aside, it's unlikely we could actually buy up enough shares to influence a stock price on our own, at least not unless you have much more money than I do.

Let's say that you and I really like Buzzard Co, a fictional marketing agency that creates a social network built on an app that makes it easy for users to spam their friends with referral links. Together, we decide to coordinate our purchase of shares, trying to time it so the stock seems to have more momentum than it really does. Then we attempt to recruit other investors, using the company's own app to spam hundreds of forums with posts extolling the benefits of Buzzard Co and explaining why its stock is such a great deal.

We might call this activist investing, but the SEC would call it price-fixing, and if it worked well enough, or if we did it often enough (with other stocks, for example), eventually we'd get in trouble.

Now let's say that it's not just you and me. Instead, we're part of a loosely affiliated group with hundreds of thousands, or maybe even millions, of people who decide to all buy shares of the same stock on the same day, coordinating our efforts through an app or network that allows everyone to be anonymous.

Most of the time, it's very difficult for groups of average traders to influence the price of stocks that trade in large volumes. But when these groups are made up of hundreds of thousands of investors, it's a different story. Now we have power, because collectively, we actually *can* drive up the price of stock. *Now* we are legion, we are Spartacus, we can do whatever we want. Who's going to stop us? It's impossible to enforce punishments against millions of people—especially when their real identities are hard to uncover.

This is essentially what happened with GameStop, a chain of failing video game stores, and later with AMC, a chain of failing movie theaters, when a merry band of self-proclaimed "degenerate" traders (who posted on Reddit using names like Nom Chompsky, NachoMan16, and TheLordJesusHimself) used a trading platform called Robinhood to drive up the price of the company's stock.

Because Robinhood was user-friendly, charged no transaction fees, and generally made it much easier to buy and sell stock options than on traditional platforms, where access had previously been limited to professional traders, this movement scaled up quickly. Pretty soon, millions of users were loosely coordinating their actions (most of which consisted of the directive "Buy more,") via a subreddit called WallStreetBets.

At the height of the craze, Robinhood halted trading in the stock, thus prohibiting many traders from getting in on the action before the price rose still higher. Public outrage ensued. Politicians including Alexandria Ocasio-Cortez ("AOC") and Senator Ted Cruz posted statements condemning the move as a form of market manipulation that favored the Wall Street investors over the independent traders: more Sheriff of Nottingham than Robin Hood and his Merry Men. (This, of course, led to a meme of its own: If both AOC and Ted Cruz are on your side, whom shall you fear?)

It turned out that the whole thing wasn't Robinhood's fault, at least according to Robinhood. You know how it goes—it was just a little misunderstanding that cost amateur traders hundreds of millions of dollars. Nothing to see here!

Whoever was to blame, the whole thing reinforced the belief that there were two separate but unequal systems: one for the ultrarich and one for everyone else.

"Oh My God, Becky, Look at That Stock"

Diving into the world of WallStreetBets (WSB) requires a crash course in phraseology. Investors are "apes," and stocks are "stonks." Profits are "tendies," short for chicken tenders. If you buy too late or fail to sell in time, you're a "bagholder."

It's a subculture where investments are highly personal, with passion and loyalty to the cause as core values. People are there to make money, sure, but they insist on doing it in a way that aligns with their belief system. "I like the stock" is a common phrase to justify why someone is buying more shares at absurdly high prices. "Stocks only go up" is another mantra, typically used even in the face of evidence to the contrary.

Forums like WSB are designed to thrive on confirmation bias. Long, impassioned posts about why a particular stock is ready to pop are upvoted, while naysayers tend to be mocked or ignored.

One of my favorite WSB ideas was the "Becky index," a fund consisting of companies favored by "white college girls." Instead of buying the S&P 500 and running the risk of owning stock in stodgy old-person brands, you could invest in $BECKY and own shares of Starbucks, Lululemon, Ulta Beauty, Planet Fitness, and Etsy.

It sounds silly, but it wasn't a bad investment: the $BECKY index ended up over 50 percent for the year.*

Safe for Work: "Loss Porn"

As with everything else in the world of Gonzo Capitalism, there were winners and losers in these battles. Lots of people bought meme stocks with money they couldn't afford to lose — then lost it when the price dropped and they sold in a panic.

If it seemed strange that millions of people were suddenly betting their life savings on struggling companies (retail stores, movie theaters, etc.), even stranger was that some of them seemed *proud* of losing lots of money.

At one point, WSB was so flooded with screenshots and

---

* Inevitably, someone proposed a counterindex known as $CHAD, containing stocks in cannabis and beer brands. Thus far, however, $BECKY has outperformed $CHAD. ("What, like it's hard?")

images of brokerage statements showing how much money someone had lost that "loss porn" became its own subcategory—one so popular that the moderators had to institute rules to keep the volume of posts under control: "Losses must be at least $5,000. Positions must be closed before posting"—i.e., paper losses don't count.

I noticed one user who posted a loss of 99.99 percent for the year. They had started with $92,000 and were down to just $10.98. *Ouch.*

And yet this investor was not deterred. Just a few months later, he was back, posting about stock options, the Federal Reserve, and how Blockbuster stock was up 700 percent.*

Was this pride rooted in a deep missional belief that led people to lose life savings out of a commitment to the cause—or did the whole thing just get away from them? Ultimately, I think the answer is a little of both. It's hard to argue that people who emptied their retirement accounts were truly happy about it. At the same time, the sense that money isn't real runs deep in WallStreetBets and related communities.

In the end, there isn't a single example or case study that's truly representative of this phenomenon. It affected many different people in both positive *and* negative ways. Just like people's views on capitalism itself, *it's complicated.*

---

* https://www.reddit.com/user/Negahnpoc.

Bartering Is Back, Sort Of

Back before money was invented, if you wanted to procure a good—rum, sugar, whale oil—you would pay for it with some other good of equivalent value, perhaps some horseshoes or a sheepskin. Fast forward roughly five thousand years, and bartering is back in vogue.

In a sense, it's another anticapitalist movement that seeks to replace the current monetary economy with a more transparent and inflation-resistant system of exchanging goods—or so its adherents claim. In practice, much of it seems to involve making videos for social media, building a following then leveraging the online fame for sponsorship money.

You might have heard the story about Kyle MacDonald, the "red paper clip guy" who famously bartered his way from a paper clip all the way up to a house. Fifteen years later, a twenty-nine-year-old from San Francisco named Demi Skipper replicated the experiment, starting with a hairpin. There's one key difference, though: Kyle's approach was old-school, while Demi's took advantage of modern networks.

With four million followers on TikTok and more than a thousand trading offers coming in via Instagram DMs each day, her mission became much more than just finding a place to live. The paper clip guy wanted to spread a message, but Demi wanted to start a revolution. As she sees it, the modern barter system creates an equal playing field in an unequal world. As she explained in an interview with *The Guardian:* "I love that it's a bit of an 'F U' to capitalism."

To her credit, Demi gave away the house that she eventually traded for—and then started all over with what she termed "season two." However, by now it had become a professional operation, if not an outright business model.

A few months later, Demi was posting on Instagram with a different message: "Do you want to refresh your space for the season ahead? I've teamed up with Rugs.com to bring you guys an amazing giveaway."

The post was tagged with a common disclosure: *Paid partnership with Rugs.com.*

In some ways, capitalism is under assault. In others, it's more resilient than ever. Hoping to get in on the huge sums of money that were being thrown around in the wake of the GameStop affair, a few institutions started exchange-traded funds (ETFs) based entirely on meme stocks.* These meme stock ETFs came with buzzworthy (if a bit on-the-nose) titles, like BUZZ, FOMO, and MEME.

Shockingly, it turned out that investing in a collection of meme stocks may not be the wisest idea. In the first half of 2022,

---

* An ETF is a lot like a mutual fund. When you buy shares in it, you get exposure to lots of different stocks.

an ETF that bundled twenty-five of the hottest stocks "based on a high social media activity score" was down more than 55 percent.

We haven't seen the last of these sensational stories. Expect more dysfunction and volatility as institutions come under scrutiny from distributed, mass groups of individuals working to coordinate their efforts.

All of which points to an obvious, bottom-line lesson: if you're tempted to throw your hat in this ring, be careful. Don't risk more than you can afford to lose.

Chapter Twelve

The New Rules of Money

CONCEPT: The tired advice of the "personal finance guru" is due for a refresh. Stop worrying about lattes, start living, and learn to take asymmetrical risks where the rewards greatly outweigh the losses.

If you've read any personal finance books, or even if you've followed a personal finance expert on social media, you might be familiar with a few words of advice. *Don't try to beat the stock market,* for instance. *Stick with index funds instead.*

Build up an emergency fund before doing anything else is another.

Save, save, save. Avoid debt, except for a mortgage, and maybe not even then. Tear up your credit cards or store them in the freezer.

It's all fairly standard, and boils down to the same recommendations that you see everywhere.

Okay, not everyone takes things as far as recommending you literally freeze your credit cards (though some do). But when it comes to investing, almost every personal finance expert has been repeating the same equation over and over for decades.

Here's another one you may have heard: To ensure that you'll be able to live comfortably forty years from now, you're supposed to identify a number you need to support your lifestyle without a regular paycheck, wherein you can withdraw 4 percent of your portfolio every year without dipping into your savings.

To get to your number, you need to live as frugally as possible, pay down any debt, and generally avoid luxuries or even anything that seems frivolous.

Do this, and one day, the theory goes, you'll be able to buy lattes with all the money you saved not buying lattes. Life goes on, at least until it doesn't.

To be fair, the standard advice isn't all bad. For most long-term stock market investing, for example, you're probably going to do better, on average, by putting your money in index funds that buy the entire market. (And it's true that the more the average person tends to tinker around by trying to pick their own winners, the lower their average return tends to be.)

However, *average* is the key word. If you want average results, follow the rules of average.

It's Time for New Rules

If you grew up in America, you almost certainly absorbed the message that if you do well in school, you'll be able to get a good job that pays good money, while your less rule-abiding class-mates are stuck working minimum-wage jobs at Walmart or Starbucks. Even if you grew up elsewhere, the odds are good that the message was similar.

One study that followed sixth graders for forty years challenged this narrative. The students who were described as "studious" when they were twelve years old did indeed end up having high-paying jobs many years later. Seems about right—but it turns out they didn't have the *highest*-paying jobs.

Those jobs went to the students who misbehaved the most, who didn't follow the rules, and who in some cases dropped out of high school or college.

Another study confirmed these results, and even found that valedictorians—who tend to be extreme rule followers—were less likely to become millionaires than their peers.

The personal finance industry is built on the experiences of people who excelled in life by following the rules. It's not surprising, therefore, that years later they have their own set of rules they expect everyone else to follow.

We've already heard plenty from them. But what can we learn from the dropouts? Instead of taking the safe path—a stable job, conservative investments, and so on—they take big risks on big ideas...and many of them are rewarded handsomely for it.

If all the advice you've been hearing for years is working for you, there's no need to change anything. But if you've made it this far in the book, I'm guessing that you're looking for strategies that don't rigidly fit into this straight-and-narrow plan.

Why abandon the rules now?, you might be wondering. There's a simple answer: The world has changed. The very nature of money has changed. And the financial technology sector ("fintech") continues to innovate, transforming the world of finance in entirely new ways.

The tired advice of personal finance experts simply doesn't hold up well with newer investments, including many mentioned in this book. As just one example, there is no "Total Stock Market Fund" for digital assets. Such a thing is currently impossible, because new assets are being created all the time. And what's the point of tearing up all your credit cards when you have constant access to all your accounts via an app on your phone?

In this chapter, I present for your consideration a new set of rules for this ever-changing world. As with any recommendations (mine or otherwise), adopt what works for you and ignore anything that doesn't.

1. Stop Trying to Take It with You

No one will tell you that their primary goal in life is to save up as much money as possible—yet many people live this way. With this mindset, accumulating money becomes the goal itself, not the means to something else.

An entire industry has been built around the idea that your ultimate mission in life is *to end up with the most money*—as though life were a game of Monopoly. Just think about how crazy it is: unless you're keeping a stash of cash under your mattress, whatever money you possess is just a number in a computer—it has no objective value until the moment you spend it. Yet this philosophy has millions of adherents who base all of their big decisions on it.

Ask yourself: If you had all the money you could ever need and more, what would you do? For many people fortunate enough to achieve this goal, the answer lies in their behavior: they simply redirect their time and talents into trying to get *more money*.

Again, most people won't freely admit this. They'll point to the fact that people are living longer after they retire, and maybe mention something about "financial independence." But if they're able to hit the magic number, they typically just revise it upward and keep striving.

Of course, you might think, *I'm not like that. All I need is [insert large number] and then I'd stop.* But the reality is you probably wouldn't, because that's not how compulsive behavior works.

When you have less money than you'd prefer, you think about getting more. When you have more, you think about...getting more. As your income expands, so do your desires, along with your definition of financial security. "But I didn't consider the taxes I'd have to pay" becomes "But I didn't consider the taxes on the fuel for the private jet."

Whenever you're feeling stressed out about money, remember that it isn't the purpose of life. Life is about relationships, experiences, growth, happiness, pain, and everything else that happens along the way.

I know what someone out there is thinking: *Well, that's easy to say for people who already have money.* And yes, it's mostly true that privilege and wealth make things easier. We don't all begin at the same starting line.

But just consider another truth: Some of the wealthiest, most privileged people are also constantly stressed about money. They may own multiple homes and take lots of fancy vacations, but they are no less miserable than anyone else.

So while there's nothing wrong with wanting more money—I mean, that's probably one reason you're reading this book—it's important to keep it in perspective.

Conveniently, this brings us to rule number two.

2. Avoid the Frugality Trap (or, Buy Experiences AND Stuff)

Personal finance literature is fond of examples that highlight how much you can save by regularly buying *one less thing* over long periods of time. These examples encourage frugal living and the resulting long, slow drip of savings: "If you give up your avocado toast and Peloton membership today, one day you'll have so much more."

Well, okay. This is true in theory. But in practice there are also a few problems—inflation, for example. As we've all seen from the postpandemic economy, when prices keep going up, the same amount of money buys less.

Also, other people are enjoying life while you're supposed to be thinking about the extra brunches you can buy thirty years from now.

If you've ever sought out advice on how to save money, you've likely come across the mantra *Buy experiences, not stuff.* The idea is that "stuff" (material possessions) provides less of a return on investment in terms of happiness than "experiences" do.

This aphorism is long overdue for a takedown. Not because it's categorically false, but because, like many memes or bumper stickers, it's just a bit too lacking in nuance. Sure, experiences *can* deliver more happiness than stuff. But the opposite can also be true. And if you've ever felt guilty when buying stuff *that makes you happy*, it's probably the fault of this philosophy.

Long ago I used to worry a lot about spending money, even when it was trivial amounts. It made me feel anxious for reasons that lacked any rationality—I wasn't going to go broke if I paid for a sandwich, but that's what it felt like.

Could I have saved a few dollars by making my lunch at home? Maybe so. All I know is, my life got a lot better when I stopped questioning every little purchase I made.

Yeah, it's cool to see the sunset—but also, sunsets are free, so there's no trade-off between seeing them and not seeing them. There's also nothing wrong with wanting to buy a new couch.

3. Stop Worrying About Debt

Millions of people live in a state of anxiety over consumer debt and student loans, and who can blame them, given how many financial gurus send the message that all debt is bad, and that the ultimate goal is to live debt-free? For millions of Americans, however, this goal falls into the category of "nice work if you can get it." Not only that, but for many of them, living without debt is not only unrealistic, but a bad idea.

What if, instead of worrying about debt, you sought to put off repaying it for as long as possible? That's what governments and other large institutions do, after all: they just keep borrowing lots of money, over and over, without worrying about the consequences. So why shouldn't you?

Some of the world's wealthiest individuals routinely take on debt. Even Mark Zuckerberg, worth approximately $110 billion at the time, took out a mortgage for his $6-million house. Larry Ellison, whose net worth hovers around $103 billion, uses a portfolio line of credit to borrow on his shares in Oracle. Depending on which media source you read, his line of credit is anywhere from $4 to $11 billion. He then uses this credit line to pay for, well, pretty much anything he wants.

It's true that Larry's living expenses are different from yours or mine: he has to cover expenses on five homes in Malibu, at least one James Bond villain–style yacht, and the sixth-largest island in Hawaii—which he now owns. The point is, Mark and Larry take on debt because they know they can earn more with their money in the market than they could if that money was tied up in "home equity." And this isn't just true for billionaires—it's also true for the rest of us.

So instead of stressing out over how quickly you can pay off debt, consider how you could put that money to work for yourself instead. Pay down or consolidate high-interest debt, sure, but some debt can be a tool to improve your life, not a burden that leaves you feeling miserable.

APPLE IS SO RICH, IT BORROWS MONEY

Apple has the most cash of any company in the world: more than $200 billion at last count. This is not the value of its investments, its market capitalization, or its Dogecoin holdings: all of that is *cash money.* Just sitting there.

Apple also has a lot of debt. More than $100 billion, in fact. Here you might wonder: Why don't they use all that cash that's just sitting there to pay off the debt?

The short answer is that they tried that once, and it didn't go well. In 1998, Apple was on the defensive, having accumulated close to $1 billion in debt. The company had famously fired Steve Jobs and later rehired him, in the hope that he would lead the company to recovery.

Jobs did just that, launching a series of revolutionary products, especially the iPhone and iPad.

Flush with these profits, the company paid off all the debt. It took a few years, but in 2004, Jobs wrote to employees announcing this triumph. "Today is a historic day," he said.

Millions of expensive computers and gadgets continued to fly off the shelves, and almost a decade later Apple became the world's first *trillion*-dollar company.

Around this time, the company started borrowing money again.

That's right. The world's premier tech giant (and one of the most successful companies in the world, period) decided to show up at the bank and fill out a credit application. Before long, it was back up to more than $500 million in debt.

If Apple were a country, it would be the eighth richest in the world. It would be worth more than Russia, Brazil, and Canada. You could take the GDP of fifteen countries in the South Pacific, including Australia and New Zealand—and Apple would be worth more than all of them put together.

Yet for all its wealth, Apple has decided to live like many consumers do: borrowing large amounts of money.

4. Learn to Take Asymmetrical Risks

Learning to take the right kinds of risks can serve you well throughout life. Some of the best risks are *asymmetrical,* which means the probability of something going catastrophically wrong is much smaller than the potential for gain.

The classic example is investing in stock options. With options, you bet on the price of a security for a predetermined future date. If you don't hit your target, you lose the opportunity to purchase at that low price—but that's all. You can never lose more than you paid. The potential gain, however, is unlimited. If the security rises (or falls, depending on the bet) 500 percent, your profit is 500 percent.

Just to be clear: I'm not saying you should become a day trader. Actively trading stock options is not for the faint of heart—but there are two larger principles here: *The right kinds of risks are worth taking,* and *inaction can sometimes be riskier than the risk itself.* Put another way, if you don't buy the lottery ticket, your odds of winning are zero.

This principle applies well beyond financial trading. Where else can we find asymmetrical risk? Let's take a career example. When Damion Taylor was laid off from his job in social media management, he decided to try his hand at the freelance life.

But rather than post his services on a platform like Fiverr, which is essentially a giant marketplace for freelancers, he had a different idea. He logged on to LinkedIn and started contacting companies that had posted job listings in search of full-time social media managers, even though Taylor wanted to work strictly on a contract basis.

His pitch was unconventional, but compelling: "Hey, I know you're looking to hire a permanent employee, but I can do this task for you on an outsourced basis for much less money." Most companies he contacted ignored him, but some listened and gave him the gig. He now earns $10,000 a month from a roster of clients that has grown to the point where he has to turn down work so he doesn't burn out.

Damion's method was a classic asymmetrical bet, with limited downside and unlimited potential. So now it's your turn: learn to identify activities that have little or no risk and the potential for 10x gains.

Ask yourself: "What could I try that wouldn't be that bad if it failed, but would be amazing if it worked?"

5. Never Pay for Something You Can Get Free

Some of life's most incredible experiences can be had for free, and I don't mean just seeing the sunrise or learning to "live simply." I'm talking about the things that most people pay money for, but that can be free for the taking—if you look for them in the right places.

For one example, my mind goes to the many, many trips I've

taken for free—or nearly for free—thanks to airline miles and hotel points.

In the spring of 2008, my quest to visit every country in the world was well underway. I'd been to something like sixty countries, but I needed to get to a lot more to hit the deadline of my thirty-fifth birthday in 2013. When I started blogging about the experience, a lot of people wanted to know how I was paying for it. *Doesn't it cost a lot to visit every country in the world?*

My first response was to point to my frugal lifestyle: I didn't own a car. I had remained debt-free. I prioritized my life to spend on what was important to me: life experiences, like travel.

All of that was true, but within the next year, I'd learn another important lesson: I didn't have to live so frugally to achieve my goal of visiting all 193 countries, because much of the cost of my flights and hotels could be covered by somebody else.

No, I didn't have sponsors. No company ever handed me a check to cover my travel, unless they were bringing me to speak at a conference. (And since by that point I needed to visit places like Somaliland and Uzbekistan, there weren't a lot of conference-hosting countries left on my list.)

What I had was a strategy to take their money in the form of credit card rewards.

At that point I'd already applied for mileage credit cards, so I knew the drill: You got a card that offered a sign-up bonus in the form of frequent flyer miles or hotel points, met the spending requirement, and collected the bonus. Then, in most cases, you either canceled the card or just put it in a drawer and forgot about it until the next year's annual fee became due.

Since I knew the basics, I decided to launch a public experiment. Over the course of a few weeks, I dutifully researched and compiled a list of all the reward cards available. Then I applied for *all of them,* or at least all I could find that offered an attractive bonus.

Within six weeks or so, I was sitting on 300,000 new airline miles and points from a range of programs. The awards were better back then, and costs were lower, too. The value of the points allowed me to visit a dozen or more countries at no extra charge, and I kept going.

Over the next few years, I did this a few more times, usually picking up six or more cards at once. The supply wasn't unlimited, but it was plentiful. I wasn't turned down for a single card, and the negative impact on my credit score was minimal. Even now, I still earn at least 200,000 or more miles a year this way.*

I chose to do this for the miles and points, which were more valuable to me than any other reward. But there are also many cards that offer all kinds of other valuable perks, including free balance transfers and no interest due for long periods of time, sometimes up to eighteen months.

---

* When I did my "Frequent Flyer Challenge," card bonuses were lower on average than they are now. These days, you can often earn 100,000 miles or points from a single card. At the same time, award charts for redemptions have also been devalued. There's inflation in the world of travel rewards, just like everywhere else.

That's effectively tens of thousands of dollars in free loans on offer, at least for anyone with good credit who can carefully manage a portfolio of accounts to ensure that the balances are paid off before the high fees kick in.

Why do card issuers offer those deals? Because they know that most people *won't* manage them well, making a good bet for the issuers.

But you don't have to be like most people. If you can manage repaying the borrowed capital on time without neglecting any payments along the way, why not take the money?

Free money can come from anywhere, if you know where to look. From free credit reports to low-interest loans from the Small Business Administration, even the government gives away money for free. Similarly, financing from banks can sometimes be forgiven or just deferred indefinitely.

Famous bank robber Willie Sutton once said, "Why rob a bank? Because that's where the money is." Maybe that was true in his time, but these days it might be easier to simply ask for money instead of taking it by force.

6. Set FIRE on Fire

The movement known as FIRE—it stands for "financial independence, retire early"—has been around for a while, but it really took off in the early days of social media. It's easy to see why: this movement has helped lots of people think about their long-term goals and take their financial planning more seriously. But it's also funneled many people into a plan and lifestyle that aren't really working for them in the here and now.

The FIRE method involves using mathematical models that usually assume a goal of $50,000 in passive income and a 4 percent withdrawal rate of a person's total capital each year. Working with fancy spreadsheets, practitioners come up with a number (sometimes called The Number) of dollars they need to accumulate before they ~~cross into nirvana~~ achieve financial independence.

A typical FIRE model looks like this:

Goal of $50,000 in passive income
Assumption of 4 percent withdrawal rate
Capital required: **$1.25 million**

In other words, to achieve passive income of $50,000 a year at a safe withdrawal rate of 4 percent, you'd need to accumulate $1.25 million in capital. If your goal is $100,000 in annual passive income, then you'd need $2.5 million, and so on (I'm simplifying a few things for this example).

So what's wrong with this? Well, it's great if you already have the money! It's also perfectly fine if you're content to spend twenty years or more in pursuit of it.

But let's say you're like lots of other people:

- You're a long way from saving $2.5 million, or whatever your magic number is.
- You want to build generational wealth instead of just live on your passive income.
- You don't want to sacrifice your entire lifestyle for the promise of wealth in the distant future.
- You *know* there's a better way, and you want to get in on it. You contribute to your retirement fund and try to make wise financial decisions. But you also wonder, *What am I missing?*

Part of what you're missing is the chance to earn higher returns from nontraditional investments, which we'll come to next.

7. Put a *Small* Percentage of Savings in Alternative Investments

I wasn't an early investor in Bitcoin (sadly), even though I'd heard of it long before it was mainstream. I don't regret not going all-in back then, because at the time of its creation, it had no guarantee of success. In fact, judging by the fact that a number of earlier digital currencies had flopped, you couldn't give it great odds.

Still, I regret not putting a *small amount* of money into it—enough that I wouldn't care if I lost it. That was my mistake: hearing about an interesting opportunity and being too skeptical to risk even a small amount.

Over the last few years, there's been no shortage of news stories predicting crypto's catastrophic demise. If you follow financial news, you've undoubtedly seen the headlines that say things like "Bitcoin plunges 60 percent from all-time highs" or "Crypto market meltdown wipes out trillions overnight."

It's true that the cryptocurrency market is prone to wild and unpredictable swings, sometimes costing investors large sums of money in a very short period of time. But a "swing," by definition, means that what goes down also goes up, and for every time Bitcoin has plunged, there have also been long periods during which it continues to rise. Even in the summer of 2022, when the coin experienced one of the steepest drops in its history, it was still trading five times higher than pre-2020 levels (meaning that if you had bought into Bitcoin prior to 2020, your assets would still be worth five times what you paid for them), and the doomsday scenarios many critics predicted never materialized.

So while the crypto market is undeniably volatile, the reality for most people is that if they had allocated even 1 percent of a typical retirement portfolio to Bitcoin in its early days, that relatively small investment would now be worth much more than everything else in their portfolio put together.

So the question isn't "Should I put my money into Bitcoin or stocks?"—it's "What are the best percentages to invest in each asset class?"

My suggestion: *Put at least 3 percent (and up to 8 percent) of your portfolio into alternative investments.* This allows you to remain fiscally conservative while still taking a chance on something new. Worst-case scenario, you lose the money. Best-case scenario, these investments far outperform any others you have.

And it could be something other than Bitcoin, obviously. Most play-to-earn games use different kinds of digital assets. Prediction markets usually use stablecoins, which are tracked with a fiat currency (like US dollars) on a 1:1 basis.

Or you could invest in digital real estate properties in the metaverse, NFTs, or whatever else comes out in the next few years. This doesn't mean that you should buy lots of random NFTs just because they look cool, or put 8 percent of your assets in any new coin that launches. Instead, you should do your research, get in early-*ish* instead of early, and keep an eye on the volatility.

New types of assets are launching all the time. What will the metaverse look like in five years, and how will it be powered, economically speaking? We just don't know.

Perhaps at some point, true market efficiency will arrive for these assets, at which point it will be better for most people to adopt a hands-off model for this kind of investing, the way they tend to do with stock index funds.

That shift will be years away, however, if it ever arrives at all.

For the foreseeable future, it *is* possible for the average person to achieve higher-than-average returns through active investing. But like any other investing, it's not without risk, so you should invest only what you can afford to lose.

8. Stake Investments for Outsize Returns

From 1920 until 2020, most people living in the US and other wealthy countries made most of their money through one of two methods: *labor* or *investments*.

Income through labor basically just means *working*, either for an employer or though self-employment. Investment returns typically include stock market dividends, bonds, and savings accounts, in addition to nonfinancial assets like gold or art.

These two methods will likely be around forever, but in 2020 a third broad method began to take root: an ingenious hybrid of the two other methods, called *staking*.

So...what is it?

In practical terms, staking is a lot like depositing money in a savings account. The bank is able to loan out your money, making money for themselves, and in turn they give you a portion of the proceeds in the form of interest.

But with staking, you deposit your money in a token or blockchain account. Put simply, this provides the liquidity a project needs to operate and grow, and you're rewarded with interest, at a much higher rate than what you'd receive with traditional investments.

And put *very* simply: stake your money, make more money.

To understand how this works, let's say that you and I have found an exciting way to bring much-needed improvements to the food delivery industry, using blockchain, artificial intelligence, and other concepts that sound cutting-edge and impressive. The only problem is that we don't have the capital to get it off the ground.

To fundraise, we make a digital token and name it HOTS, for *hotcakes*. But for our project to become feasible and stable, it needs liquidity—we need a lot more people to trade with it. Otherwise, it will be vulnerable to "whales," who deposit large sums of money, then abruptly take their profits and run. Without liquidity, our hotcakes project won't make it off the griddle.

How do we get people to provide the liquidity we need to stabilize our token? Well, unfortunately, people won't work for free. That's where investors come in: we invite individual investors to stake funds to HOTS in exchange for interest and rewards. Everyone profits from our tasty token!

Two Ways to Win

Soon after I started experimenting with staking protocols, I began to understand one of their most powerful features: *you earn rewards even when the price of the underlying security drops.* These rewards have the potential to increase your overall returns—or at least offset your losses if the market moves against you.

I experienced this in early 2022, when Bitcoin dropped more than 40 percent from its all-time high. Most crypto markets are still highly dependent on Bitcoin's price; when it falls, everything else tends to follow. Like millions of others, in the space of a few days I saw some investments decline *more* than 40 percent.

Not ideal!

The standard advice during market free falls is not to panic, to stay the course and wait for prices to eventually rebound. And in the meantime, your staked assets will continue to accrue rewards.

This happens to be good advice.

Every day, no matter how sad the overall market looked, I received more rewards in the form of tokens in my account. I wasn't happy about losing (at least on paper) so much of my original investment, but the bright side was seeing more and more tokens being added to my holdings automatically.

I did the math and realized that thanks to staking rewards, with enough time I could still come out ahead *even if the price never recovered.*

Granted, that wouldn't be the preferred outcome. I got into this kind of aggressive investing to earn outsize returns, not to match the payout rate of government bonds. But it was still so much better than investing only in assets that didn't provide any sort of interim rewards. That is the true power of staking. You have two possible ways to win: through price appreciation *and* through daily staking rewards.

STAKING: GETTING STARTED

The easiest way to get started with staking is through a centralized exchange like Coinbase, Binance, or Crypto.com. Most of them are happy to help you do this—extremely happy, in fact, because they take a cut of everything you earn.

I did this with Ethereum, the world's second-largest cryptocurrency. I didn't realize until I had my ETH locked up with Coinbase that they took a 25 percent commission on the returns—and once I'd made the choice, there was no going back. Not only was I earning less and less as more people entered the staking pool, I had to pay Coinbase a big chunk of those returns.

When you're starting out, though, the exchanges add value by making a complex transaction easy.

If you do decide to get into staking, here are a few other tips to help ease your way.

Go slow, then ramp up as you feel confident. As with every other strategy in this book, don't jump in headfirst. Approach it with caution and take some time to learn about it.

If you have a significant portfolio, *designate a small percentage toward staking.* Staking is a medium-risk investment strategy. It's not as aggressive as going all-in with the latest meme stock, and not as conservative as keeping all your money in index funds.

Put your eggs in a few baskets. Don't be a maximalist (someone who puts everything in one investment), but don't spread yourself too thin, either. Knowledge is cumulative, especially in a new industry with so much developing so quickly. With new knowledge come new opportunities.

Once you understand more, leave the exchange. As mentioned, the exchanges typically charge a hefty commission in exchange for convenience. If I'd better understood the process, I could have skipped Coinbase and gone elsewhere. If you don't value the convenience of an exchange, you can head straight for the DIY route and save on fees.

What Could Go Wrong?

A guy I knew through one of the Discords I was monitoring once wrote to me excitedly about a strategy he'd devised. He sent me a password-protected Google Sheet that claimed to show a method of investing that provided a guaranteed annual return of 70 percent.

This astonishingly high return was achievable, he claimed, through a series of convoluted moves. You had to stake funds in one protocol, borrow against the capital, and then allocate those funds to another token. Because of...some form of mathematical alchemy I didn't understand...you'd be able to earn this incredible amount of return with no risk.

For the record, my friend is not the type of person who believes that the government faked the moon landing, or that the Covid vaccine contains a tracking chip. But he somehow did not feel the same skepticism that most investors would upon hearing about a "guaranteed" 70 percent annual return.

Indeed, this strategy turned out to be vulnerable to two massive problems he didn't foresee. First, when most of the market crashed, the underlying tokens experienced a huge drop in value. Second, the Harmony blockchain in which these tokens resided was attacked by hackers from North Korea, who stole more than $100 million.

Money may not be real, but this particular form of fake money ended up being worth a lot less than expected.

The point is, investing in digital assets is not without risk. For one thing, there's no federal agency that insures your money. If you keep money in a US bank account, the FDIC guarantees that up to $250,000 of it will be safe. And some other countries have similar protections.

No matter where you live, however, you probably won't have any insurance or protection for digital assets you deposit. And therein lies the downside of decentralized governance: there's no centralized authority to step in if you've fallen victim to a hack or a scam.

The *Squid Game* Token Where Everyone ~~Dies~~ Goes Broke

Sometimes developers even hack their own projects from within, drain users' accounts, and run off with the money. This is known as a rug-pull, because users rarely see it coming. Surprise! Your account is empty. (Yes, the calls really do come from inside the house.)

On the heels of Netflix's hit show *Squid Game*, an anonymous group set up $SQUID, a token that promised its holders the ability to participate in a cool *Squid Game*–themed play-to-earn game.

Except there was no game—or maybe there was, but the anonymous creator was the only one playing it, and its primary objective was to steal money from the players. Less than a month after its debut, they cashed out. $SQUID dropped from $2,861 in value to *almost zero*.

The 43,000 $SQUID holders were left with nothing, and the anonymous creators walked away with $3.36 million.

And that was that. The whole affair got little attention, aside from a few online articles about the rise and fall of $SQUID, and no real attempt at recovery or prosecution.

What could be done? The token's creators were anonymous and had covered their tracks well. "Sorry again for any inconvenience been made for you," they said in a parting message.

In the case of $SQUID, the red flags were hard to miss: the website and white paper describing the project were filled with wild claims and grammatical errors, and on the coin's Telegram channel, only the project's creators were allowed to post messages. It was also pretty clear that neither Netflix nor the show's creator had anything to do with the project.[*]

But many times, the warning signs aren't nearly as clear. Malicious project creators often have "tells" (see above), but the legions of hackers who constantly monitor the code and smart contracts these projects run on, searching for vulnerabilities, are undetectable. If something wasn't written properly at the outset—or if a feature added later contains an unnoticed security weakness— that vulnerability can often be exploited for profit.

The good news is that these worries keep a lot of coders up at night. Honest project creators know that keeping users' funds safe is mission critical, so they hire smart people and pay for frequent code audits.

Web3 is a model example of a system that needs chaos in order to thrive and flourish. It's a quality that *Black Swan* author Nassim Taleb calls "antifragile." Just as every plane crash makes

---

[*] As one commentator put it: "If they'd watched the show, they would have known there could only be one winner."

the airline industry safer in the long run because of the knowledge gained through investigation, every digital currency breach is studied to improve the security of future projects.

This is another reason why getting in early-*ish* with a promising digital currency or blockchain-based project is often a better strategy than being the very first. When you're really early, you're more at risk of getting grifted or hacked. Once the project has attracted some attention and been around for a while (but not too long), and as the team that runs it builds a track record, it's less likely to be a scam.

Don't Forget It's All Taxable

Losing all your money to a scammer is the worst-case scenario. In the best-case scenario, you have a different problem. Now that you've made a lot of money, chances are you owe a lot of it in taxes.

Just as you need to pay tax for the other two forms of income — employment and capital gains — you're not off the hook when it comes to staking. This sounds like a good problem to have (and it *is*, overall), but it can still create issues.

A common situation: Your favorite token has a great year, and you earn a ton of rewards for it. This means, of course, that you're going to owe a good amount of tax on those rewards.

You assume that when the time comes to file your return,

you'll withdraw whatever you need to pay the bill. After all, you don't want to withdraw profits too early—you'd miss out on more returns!

But then, in a stark reversal, your favorite coin drops in value in January. Well, now you still owe a lot of money to the government, and you have a lot less money with which to pay.

The best way to avoid this unfortunate scenario is to *take profits* toward the end of a profitable year. As I learned several times over during my year of experiments, if you don't plan to take profits, you could end up worse off in several ways.

"ERROR: UNABLE TO CALCULATE APY"

When I was learning about decentralized finance (DeFi), I came across something called yield farming, a complex activity that involves staking pairs of coins to earn high amounts of interest. How much interest? Some projects offered 300 percent or more!

That number is an APR (annual percentage rate), but if you compound your rewards, the APY (annual percentage *yield*) can be much higher.

Running the numbers on APY is a little complicated, so it helps to use an online tool. Many such tools exist, but I soon ran into a problem: Most of the free tools I found online simply couldn't compute the yield on such high returns. Typically, they returned an error message ("Unable to calculate APY" or similar).

It was as though the calculator was saying, "Whoa, slow down!" One could interpret that as a metaphor for DeFi in general, but at the same time, when did anyone ever complain about yields being *too high*?

I did finally find a tool that worked well, or at least that didn't self-combust when I tried to run projections.* The lesson: even if you can compound APR into APY, it's still good to take profits periodically in order to avoid big losses.

* https://www.thecalculatorsite.com/finance/calculators/daily-compound-interest.php.

For those who are still wondering if there's a case to be made for investing in digital assets, there is! At least, there's a case for a cautious approach in which these assets don't constitute too much of your overall savings portfolio.

The tired advice from the personal finance industry is due for a refresh. Remember: average advice works for some people, some of the time. But if you want above-average results, you'll need to go further.

So stop worrying, start living, and learn to take risks where the rewards greatly outweigh the losses.

— Postscript —

As I was finishing up this book, the rappers Drake and 21 Savage released a new album. According to their press materials and social media posts, the album was accompanied by a flurry of publicity: they were on the cover of *Vogue*, they performed on *Saturday Night Live*, they were interviewed on NPR's *Tiny Desk* program and on Howard Stern. They capped it all off by winning Grammy Awards for album of the year.

The catch was that *none of it was real*. All the hype was manufactured. There was no *SNL* appearance, the *Vogue* cover posted to Instagram was Photoshopped, the clip from the supposed Howard Stern interview was a deepfake, and that year's Grammys had just taken place before the album came out. It was all a clever marketing stunt.

The campaign was so well done, however, that it had much the same effect as if all those things had actually happened. Howard Stern played the fake interview clip on his real show, and NPR's *Tiny Desk* congratulated the rappers—and even extended an invitation to "do it for real"—in a post on its social accounts.

I thought about this story while editing the final chapters of the book. Drake and 21 Savage's album was just like most things of value in today's economy: bold, creative, and not real until it actually was.

What ingenuity will Gonzo Capitalism unleash next? Only time will tell. As for me, I moved on from Britney Spears, but I kept making bets elsewhere. During the midterms, I made $400 betting against Herschel Walker in the Georgia Senate campaign. Thanks, Herschel! Meanwhile, PredictIt continued its legal battle with the Commodity Futures Trading Commission (CFTC). The site may or may not be in existence at the time you're reading this, but if it isn't, there will surely be many other ways to make money by betting on the future.

The play-to-earn gaming world was hit hard during the crypto crash, with many projects nose-diving into a state of life support. Some games did better than others, though, and I kept investing in virtual animals that completed daily chores in exchange for more tokens. Now, in addition to being grateful in retrospect that esports arrived too late for my twenty-year-old self, I think it's probably good that blockchain gaming wasn't perfect at first. Otherwise, I might never have finished writing this book.

In the months since, the growth of AI continued to accelerate, with new advances coming out all the time. Unfortunately, AI writing tools still weren't quite good enough to write this book for me in time for my deadline. (OR WERE THEY??)

I heard from more and more people working multiple jobs simultaneously, or sometimes taking jobs only for the paycheck, without doing much work at all. And through it all, MrBeast kept making videos. *Money printer go brrrr.*

Speaking of money printers: after Sam Bankman-Fried, the young founder of a crypto exchange called FTX, saw his $20-billion fortune eviscerated in a day, he was extradited from his penthouse apartment in the Bahamas. Before being taken into custody, he gave a series of bizarre interviews, including one in which he claimed to despise books. "I would never read a book," he told a reporter. "I don't want to say no book is ever worth reading, but I actually do believe something pretty close to that. I think, if you wrote a book, you fucked up, and it should have been a six-paragraph blog post."

Personally, I like books a lot, and I'm fortunate to work with others who feel the same way. My agent David Fugate and I have now been together for eight books and counting. David suggested that I make an AI art cover for this one, but it turned out that I'm good only at pencil drawings of cats drinking milkshakes. The real-life humans at Macmillan Publishers in the UK did a much better job. Ranka Stević, Olya Iver, and some of the team from Little, Brown Spark helped as well.

My editor, Talia Krohn, worked especially hard on this manuscript. Applying our most skeptical editing filters, together we removed almost every reference to *Wild West*. (I'm sorry to say there were many in the first draft.) We also used the word *disruption* only once...okay, maybe twice.

Special thanks go to Jedd Chang, Nat Eliason, Jonathan Fields, Jolie Guillebeau, Mary Guillebeau, Nick Hajal, Matt

— Postscript —

Levine, Sara Mohtashamipour, Lisa Sansouci, and David Van Veen. Each of them helped in an important way.

Last but certainly not least, I really do feel grateful to be able to write books and speak with so many interesting people. If you've been reading my work for a while, my greatest expression of thanks goes to you. (If you're new, subscribe to my weekly newsletter at ChrisGuillebeau.com.)

I know that not everything in this book will be appropriate for everyone. I trust that you're smart enough to decide for yourself what works for you and what doesn't. Whatever you do, just remember: The many systems you encounter throughout life are designed for average people. If you want average results, follow an average plan.

At some point in recent history, the global economy stopped making sense—or at least so it seemed. Though there were many twists and turns along the way, the world of Gonzo Capitalism represents a turning point in the history of money.

Looking back at the pandemic economy can feel like a dream sequence in a movie. You might wonder, *Did all of that really happen? Also—is it over?*

The definitive answer would be: Yes, as strange as it was, it did in fact happen.

And is it over?

Not at all. It's just beginning.

Chris Guillebeau
December 31, 2022

Index

Index

Index

Index

Index

Index

Index

Index

Index

CHRIS GUILLEBEAU is the *New York Times* bestselling author of *The $100 Startup, The Happiness of Pursuit, Side Hustle,* and other books. During a lifetime of self-employment, he visited every country in the world before his thirty-fifth birthday. Chris writes for a small army of remarkable people at ChrisGuillebeau .com. Follow him on Twitter (@chrisguillebeau), or on Instagram (@193countries), or listen to his daily podcast, *Side Hustle School,* at SideHustleSchool.com.